THE WINDOWS
OF
ST. MICHAEL'S

LIFT HIGH THE CROSS

Illustrations and Commentaries
on the Significance of
Christian Symbols in the
Stained Glass Windows
St. Michael's Episcopal Church

Research by
Harriet T. Hill

Window Design by
Mary Partricia Stumpf

Text on Nave Windows by
James F. Day, Ph.D.

Edited by
Hayne Palmour III, Ph.D.
The Rev. E.T. Malone, Jr.

Text / Edited by
Harriet T. Hill

Photography by
Harriet T. Hill
Joy Batchelor

Published for
St. Michael's Episcopal Church
by Marblehead Publishing
Raleigh, NC

D1242568

THE WINDOWS OF ST. MICHAEL'S

Stained Glass Window Committee

Harriet T. Hill, Chairperson

Maurice N. Courie, M.D.

Wright T. Dixon, Jr.

Robert C. Greene

Ann S. Hall

Peggy S. Manly

Hayne Palmour III, Ph.D

June, 1997

Special thanks to Susan W. Little
Financial Secretary

THE WINDOWS OF ST. MICHAEL'S

TABLE OF CONTENTS

PREFACE

In August of 1982, a committee was formed to evaluate the possibilities for placing stained glass windows in St. Michael's Church. Over a period of four years, this evolved into a series of studio and designer explorations, coupled with extensive research into appropriate themes and orderly sequences of designs for the 26 windows in the nave and the two small windows in the narthex of the church.

The initial ideas turned into the final concept: there would be a sequential story told, featuring the liturgy professed in the Episcopal Church. It would be done by incorporating the seasonal colors and using universally accepted Christian symbols to depict key elements of the liturgical message. The history, significance, and appropriate use of each symbol was considered, and a unifying overall pattern for presentation of the symbols was selected. Both thematically and artistically, each window could stand on its own, yet be an integral part of the whole.

The Committee agreed with the premise that any stained glass window must support the concept of a place of worship—and should teach. St. Michael's was designed with the idea that one should enter the church and want to kneel down and worship God. Clearly, the windows needed to reinforce that same feeling.

Finally, a Raleigh artist with a sound understanding of this concept was engaged to create the final designs. She was able to capture the innate spirituality of the message and to understand that stained glass magnifies the Light of God with the refraction of light through colored glass.

It is appropriate here to quote William Willett, a second generation owner of The Willett Stained Glass Studios in Philadelphia, fabricators of our windows. He wrote in 1918:

> It is only when reverence guides the hand that the healing power, of which the fathers spoke, steals through the storied pane. That school of art which creates its own god, never has and never can produce a high type of art, for the breath of God is beauty, and He expresses Himself in order and harmony.

It is hoped that these stained glass windows in St. Michael's Church will bring a deeper understanding of our faith, and a profound sense of joy, peace and harmony to all those who experience them.

Harriet T. Hill, Chairperson
Stained Glass Window Committee
St. Michael's Episcopal Church

Raleigh, N. C.
June, 1997

Nave windows dedicated June 7, 1987
Chapel window dedicated Trinity Sunday, May 29, 1988
Narthex window dedicated October 26, 1997

THE WINDOWS OF ST. MICHAEL'S

by

James F. Day, Ph. D.

INTRODUCTION

As long as mankind has been worshipping, artists have sought to praise God in painting, sculpture, architecture, music and literature. To religious artists, this work is primarily an act of praise to God, for artistic creation is itself a microcosm of God's own Creation. In creating a work of art, the artist worships by imitating in a small way the great creative activity of God. When art is conceived to draw men to God and to praise the Creator Himself, our own response is not only to bless God, it is to be blessed ourselves.

From Solomon's Temple to the great European cathedrals to parish churches such as this one, the worship of God has been adorned by works of art praising Him and edifying His faithful people. In a very real sense, such works of art are the alms one age gives to another. Just as the Church is enjoined to charity in providing for the physical needs of her charges, so she provides spiritual alms for their souls as well. Not only out of civic or professional pride were the great Gothic churches built in Europe, but art and architecture were carefully planned to reflect the glory of God and to instruct and delight the people in God's majesty and love.

Ecclesiastical art bears witness to the faith and understanding of the Church in past ages; it serves as a link physically binding the Church throughout all ages into one. The prayers formed in a church's glass and stone, in her music and poetry, articulate the Universal Church's longing for her Lord, and all who are moved by such human acts of creation are in a real sense drawn to Charity at its source.

The Tradition of Stained Glass

The art of the glazier, stained glass, is a particularly suitable medium for expressing the love of God. First of all, it is almost entirely a Christian medium in its origin. The oldest complete stained glass windows, the "Five Prophets" in Augsburg Cathedral, date to the end of the eleventh century. Even earlier references exist dealing with glazed windows in churches, and some ancient glass fragments of such windows have survived. Though colored glass has existed for centuries, and glass mosaics have served both sacred and secular purposes East and West, it is clear that the widespread use of colored glass window pictures is a Christian development.

Certainly it is with the Church that stained glass reached its zenith, particularly beginning with the development of Gothic architecture. Gothic buildings did not need the massive walls required by the earlier Romanesque style. As a result, large windows became possible. Anyone who has stood before "Nótre Dame de la Belle Verrière" in Chartres, or anyone who has been amazed by the "wall" of glass windows around the upper chapel of St. Louis' Saint Chappelle in Paris, or anyone who has delighted in the grisaille "Five Sisters" of York Minster knows how brilliantly successful such expanses of medieval colored glass can be.

But most importantly, the tradition of such art in the service of God did not end in the Middle Ages. Successive ages of glaziers have continued the tradition, sometimes self-consciously imitating earlier styles with varying success; sometimes experimenting in the idiom of the age. This experimentation, too, is important, especially if a work of art is to become one age's spiritual legacy to another. In ecclesiastical art, one must always remember the great tradition that has been inherited from the past.

In our own century, artists working in glass at places such as the National Cathedral of SS. Peter and Paul in Washington and Coventry Cathedral in England have created remarkable stained glass to God's glory in a very modern idiom. One may prefer Chartre's "Nótre Dame de la Belle Verrière" to Washington's "Space Window" or one may not; the important thing is that each generation bears witness to God in its own language, thus refreshing and enriching the Christian tradition in every age.

It is this tradition that St. Michael's Church joins by glazing the church's windows with stained glass. What better legacy could a church leave than its witness to God's splendor by sermons in symbols, pictures painted with light itself, the medium with which Our Lord so clearly identifies Himself?

Inception of St. Michael's Nave Windows

It is to honor the Light of the World that St. Michael's has commissioned these stained glass windows. The project had been suggested for several years, but it was not until 1982 that the first steps were taken with the formation of a Stained Glass Window Committee, under the leadership of Harriet T. Hill.

The initial sketches for the windows, researched and designed by Mrs. Hill, were planned to be simple in order to harmonize with the modern architecture of the church. The scheme, based on the seasons of the Church Year, uses the various symbols associated with each season to emphasize its place in the Christian story. Each window has an appropriate plant at the bottom, symbols of the relevant event in the center, and a different cross at the top. This basic pattern thus unifies the sequence of the windows and gives them a cohesive effect.

Many consultations followed. Artistic help has come from Mary Patricia Stumpf, a Raleigh artist, and from Dr. Charlotte Brown (Mrs. Eugene W.), Architectural Historian and Director of the Visual Arts Center at North Carolina State University in Raleigh. Along with this invaluable aid, The Willet Stained Glass Studios of Philadelphia and its president, Crosby Willet, have worked on the project almost from its inception. Further assistance on the liturgical and symbolic significance of the windows has come from Berta Allen Summerall (Mrs. J. J.) and Dr. James F. Day, who also suggested the sequential layout of the windows. The final artistic designs were done by Mary Patricia Stumpf (Mrs. Dale R.).

The result is a series of twenty-eight windows, all but two symbolizing the Church Year. The cycle begins with Advent, the first window on the left as one enters the nave [1]. The sequence then follows clockwise around the church to end with the first window on the right [26], the Sunday Next Before Advent (also called the Feast of Christ the King). The effect is to surround the church with the Church Year itself, reminding the congregation of the constant round of prayer offered up by the liturgy as well as the specific events of the history of our salvation and the Church's life.

In designing this sequence, it has not been possible to include all the observances of the

Church Year. Accordingly, many occasions are subsumed in other windows or are omitted altogether. For instance, the observances of individual saints have largely been subsumed under All Saints, though as befitting the dedication of the church, St. Michael is commemorated in the Michaelmas Window [24] as well as The St. Michael's Church Window [27] in the narthex.

The choice of symbols was also difficult—iconography is not a science but an art, and much depends on the artistic designer's invention. In the following pages, explanation of the various symbols is given. Those who view these windows may find their own worship increased by understanding and joy as they see around them images of their faith emblazoned in color and light.

Advent is above all a season of expectation, of waiting. Thus, though the most frequent Western tradition is to assign **purple** to it as the appropriate color, it is not quite as penitential a season as Lent. In this window the traditional ideas of Advent's preparation for the coming of the Christ are combined with the symbols of the historical forerunner of Christ, St. John the Baptist. Thus the **carob plant**, which gave the "locusts" eaten by St. John in the wilderness, appears at the bottom of the window.

Under the cross, the **Lamb on the book** refers to St. John's *"Ecce Agnus Dei"* ("Behold the Lamb of God"), which St. John applied to Christ, the Word of God. This Latin inscription is frequently an attribute of St. John the Baptist in Christian art.

The seven seals on the book recall those in the book mentioned in the fifth chapter of the Revelation of the other St. John (St. John the Divine), where the Lamb of God is declared worthy to receive all honor, glory and blessing.

The **tablet of the Law** refers to Christ's fulfillment of the Law, and the **Rising Sun** to Christ as the Sun of Righteousness or the "Dayspring from on high." The **key*** is the Key of David: "Lead forth from prison those who lie in chains, who dwell in darkness and the shadow of death." **Alpha and Omega** under the **Tau Cross** (attributed to Moses' staff) refer to Christ the Beginning and the End, for though he was born in time, yet is He Lord of Time.

*Given to the Glory of God and in Loving Memory of
Anne Elizabeth Cox Worth, September 15, 1920 - August 4, 1986
by Colvin McAlister Worth*

I.

---

* Also borrowed from the traditional "O Antiphons" which the Church historically used for the days just before Christmas and which have been preserved in the hymn "O Come, O Come, Emmanuel."

2.

Violets and Strawberries are often used together to suggest humility and righteousness; here they remind us of Our Lord's humility in His Incarnation and birth. It is the lowliness of that origin that this window emphasizes: the Light of the World, for whose birth in a stable (or a **cave**), left His rightful place and condescended to dwell among us.*

With the **manger** and Greek **"Chi Rho"** monogram for Christ are the two animals associated traditionally with Christ's birth, the **humble ass** and the **patient ox**. These animals regularly appear in Nativity scenes. The ass particularly is an animal associated with Our Lord, for it is upon such an animal that Mary traveled into Bethlehem and that Jesus rode into Jerusalem.

Reminding us of Our Lord's humility by contrasting it with His holiness, the **Cross Botonnée**—with its three-lobed arms—suggests the glory of the Trinity. It also may imply the budding of a flower, as in Christ's new creation.

*Given to the Glory of God and in Memory of
Roger I. Wall, M.D., August 29, 1909 - May 21, 1980
by Phyllis Stier Wall*

* The seasonal color, **white**, symbolizes innocence, purity, truth and joy.

NATIVITY, ANGELS AND SHEPHERDS

White is the joyous color of Christmas and Easter, along with other great feasts of celebration.

It is the legend of the **Glastonbury Thorn** that makes a connection between Easter and Christmas, for this type of hawthorn blooms in December and in May. Here it may remind us that the proclamation of the angels led not only to Bethlehem but also to Golgotha. The blossoms supposedly grew from the thornwood staff of St. Joseph of Arimathea, who, after burying Christ, finally came to Glastonbury in England. In the Middle Ages, Glastonbury was the site of a great religious house of wealth and power.

The Angelic announcement, **"Gloria in Excelsis Deo"** above the **shepherds' crooks,** indicates the hurried departure of the shepherds to Bethlehem to see Him for whom Angels sing.

The cross is a **Cross Clechée** (meaning "key"), suggestive of Jesus as being the key of salvation.

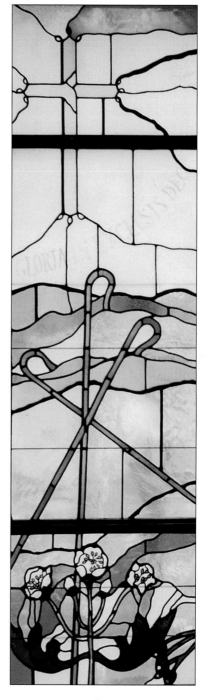

Given to the Glory of God and in Thanksgiving for the Lives of
Mr. & Mrs. Harris W. Haskett and Mr. & Mrs. Earl L. Brown
by Lawrence Kemster Brown and Margaret Haskett Brown
and in Honour of
Mr. & Mrs. William Frederick Greenwell
by Norwood Foye Crawford and Anne Greenwell Crawford

3·

THE HOLY INNOCENTS

4.

"I n Rama was there a voice heard, lamentation and weeping, and great mourning: Rachel weeping for her children, and would not be comforted, because they are not." The massacre of the **Holy Innocents**, the children slain on Herod's orders in his attempt to kill the infant Jesus, is commemorated by the Church on **December 28.**

The symbols of martyrdom, the **sword** and the **palm branches** (heavenly victory over death) are combined with the celestial crown intertwined with traditional martyrs' **lilies and roses** (for purity and for the blood that was shed). The purity and innocence associated with lilies is echoed by the **lilies of the valley** that relate to Advent and to the Blessed Virgin, who, like the mothers of the Holy Innocents, would also mourn her Child.

The arms of the **Cross Cercelée** may suggest a cradle, though it should be pointed out that much symbolism, especially in various types of crosses, often arises *after* someone has designed a new cross for decoration.*

However, the **dark, blood-red color** for the Feasts of Martyrs *is* symbolic and is used to commemorate the day on which the martyr or martyrs died, for that day is their "heavenly birthday." A lighter shade of red represents the joy of those who sacrifice in the name of Jesus.

Given to the Glory of God and in loving Memory of Katharine Smith Borden and Katherine William Talcott by Benjamin McNinch Currin and Mary Borden Currin

---

* Here, for instance, the Cross Moline, of which the **Cross Cercelée** is a variant, is a heraldic device thought to be based on the shape of the center iron of a millrind rather than anything remarkably symbolic.

EPIPHANY, THE HOLY NAME OF JESUS

The 1979 *Book of Common Prayer* designates **January 1** as "The Holy Name of Our Lord Jesus Christ." Originally this Feast was called the Circumcision of Christ. The Holy Name, as a devotion, generally was observed by the late Medieval English Church on August 7th, the day after the traditional Feast of the Transfiguration of Our Lord. Devotion to the Holy Name of Jesus (as the only Name given for salvation) "at which every knee should bow" is thus combined with the idea of Circumcision in Our Lord's fulfillment of the Law.

Here the monogram of the Holy Name, **IHC** in Greek, is shown below the **Epiphany* Star** which points to it, suggesting the coming of the Magi to worship.

The **Epiphany Season** begins on **January 6**, utilizing representative colors of **white** (light and purity) and **green** (new life).

At the bottom of the window, one of the gifts of the Magi, **frankincense**, recalls worship in the Temple, for it was there that it was burned on the Altar of Incense.

The **Eastern (or Russian) Orthodox Cross** appears here reminding us that it was to Wise Men from the East that Christ was first made manifest to the gentiles.

Given to the Glory of God and in Memory of
Nathan Thomas
May 22, 1916 - August 1, 1981
by Nancy Sugg Thomas

5.

---

* **Epiphany** is a Greek word; *epi* means upon, and *phanein* means showing. The five points of the star presage the five wounds of Christ at His crucifixion.

Continuing the theme of worshipping the Incarnate Christ is the Feast of the Epiphany, "The Manifestation of Christ to the Gentiles," which commemorates the coming of the Magi to worship the infant Jesus, thus making known the salvation of the world to gentiles as well as Jews.

The **three crowns** relate to the tradition that the Magi were three Kings, though neither the number nor the rank of the Magi, or Wise Men, is found in scripture. We do know that the Magi brought three **gifts: gold, frankincense, and myrrh**. These were meritorious in themselves, though we value as well their appropriateness for Our Lord: gold for adorning a King, frankincense for worshipping God, and myrrh for burying a man.

Below the gifts, the **myrrh plant**, used for preparing bodies for burial, also recalls the love imagery of the Song of Songs, for this aromatic gum is associated with both death and love.

The **Cross Crosslet** is said to symbolize the spread of the Gospel to the four corners of the earth, the light "to lighten the gentiles."

Given to the Glory of God and in Thanksgiving for
Chad and Will Davis
by Mr. & Mrs. Charles B. Davis III

The 1979 *Book of Common Prayer* sets aside the First Sunday after the Epiphany to remember the Baptism of Our Lord, and it is this event, along with the Sacrament of Baptism itself, that we contemplate here. The **Descending Dove**,* the form in which the Holy Ghost was manifested at Christ's baptism by St. John the Baptist, hovers over a traditional symbol of Baptism, a **shell** pouring out water.**

Although Baptism by immersion is apparently the early form of Christian Baptism, we see most commonly in Christian art a later tradition: Christ standing in the Jordan and St. John the Baptist pouring water over Him. Associated with Christian Baptism, though inapplicable specifically to the sinless Lamb of God, is **hyssop**. "Psalm 51," the Miserere, is one of the classic references for this cleansing attribute of hyssop: "Thou shalt cleanse me with **hyssop** and I shall be clean."

The eight points forming the **Maltese Cross** here refer to the idea of rebirth or regeneration; the seven days of the old creation beginning again, or Christ rising on the eighth day after His entry into Jerusalem. Many baptismal fonts are therefore eight-sided, symbolic of this rebirth.

Given to the Glory of God and in Thanksgiving for Eternal Life by James Allen Hill, Jr. and Harriet Tomlinson Hill

7.

---

* A **three-rayed nimbus** around the head of a Christian symbol indicates that the symbol represents a divine being.
** An **escallop shell**, traditionally, is a symbol of purification.

THE MIRACLES OF OUR LORD

8.

For the Gospel at Eucharist, the traditional lectionary for the Sundays after the Epiphany incorporated various miracles of Christ. Although these associations have been somewhat reworked in the 1979 *Book of Common Prayer*, this window, in honor of Christ's miracles, is still very appropriate as a bridge between Epiphany and Lent.

Christ's miracles are perhaps the aspect of His ministry which, along with the parables, can best be shown in art. Here Christ's life between the cradle and the cross is evoked by signs of His own signs, the miracles which He gave that He might be believed.

His first miracle, changing water into wine at the wedding in Cana (represented by **earthenware jars and grapes**), is found in St. John's Gospel. With the wine jars, the **loaves and fish** recall the feeding of the five thousand, which is common to all the Gospels. Here Our Lord made a small boy's meal of five loaves and two fish feed a great multitude of people, with twelve baskets left over.

Christ's healing miracles are suggested by the plant, **balm,** chosen for the bottom of this window. Balm is associated with healing, as we find in the Book of Jeremiah: "Is there no balm in Gilead?"

The Latin **Cross Fleurée**, with its flowering arms, is held to suggest the mature Christian.

Given to the Glory of God, and in Loving Appreciation of Their Parents
Mr. & Mrs. Earl Newton Howard
and
Mr. & Mrs. Henry Harding Latham
by Mr. & Mrs. Robert Earl Howard

The season of Lent, shrouded in **purple** or the unbleached linen of "Lenten array," is the Church's time for repentance and reflection.

The season begins with Ash Wednesday, in which **ashes** made from last year's Palm Sunday **palms** are imposed on the foreheads of many Christians with the reminder that they are dust and shall return to dust. With the **ashes and their box** is the **alabaster container of spikenard* perfume** which Mary the sister of Martha and Lazarus broke open to anoint Our Lord's feet, thus anointing Him symbolically for His burial, as the imposition of ashes reminds us of our own. This Mary is traditionally identified with St. Mary Magdalene, although the 1979 *Book of Common Prayer* observes St. Mary Magdalene and Mary and Martha separately. Still, the association with the Magdalene gives the spikenard an interconnection with that saint's repentance. The account of the woman with the precious ointment is in all the Gospels except St. Luke's. While there is some variation in each telling, all include the disciples' grumbling over the waste of such expensive perfume; but Jesus Himself commends the woman, saying that her act will always be a memorial to her.

At the bottom of the window, **rue** is also suggestive of repentance. Shakespeare's *Hamlet* refers to it as the "herb o' grace," and it is used even today in sprinkling holy water.

The **Latin Cross** here is wreathed with thorns and flowers as a foretelling that the coming Passion of Our Lord will be followed by His Resurrection.

Given to the Glory of God and in Loving Memory of
Mr. & Mrs. Cleveland Charles Mangum
and
Mr. & Mrs. Walter Franklin Burgiss
by Mr. & Mrs. Michael David Mangum

9.

---

* **Spikenard blossoms** are depicted behind the alabaster box.

THE ANNUNCIATION

The **white** joy of the Annunciation, long called "Lady Day," usually cuts into the purple gloom of Lent like a shaft of sunlight on a cloudy day. *Usually* because the Feast can fall in Holy Week or Easter Week, which take precedence. Then the Feast, normally **March 25th**, is transferred to a later day. The date for the Feast was figured on the traditional date for Christmas, although that in itself is a mere historical convenience, as it falls nine months before December 25th. Nevertheless, in March we celebrate the announcement by the angel Gabriel to the Blessed Virgin Mary that she would conceive Our Lord.

Thus, although the feast is one of Our Lord's Incarnation, it is His Mother's monogram that appears above the **almond plant** associated with her reception of divine favor.* This miracle also has come to symbolize the Virgin Mother of Our Lord, who miraculously brought forth Christ.

Above the **monogram**, in which can be traced the letters **"MARIA,"**** are the **twelve stars and crescent moon** of the "woman clothed with the sun" who gives birth to the Dragon's enemy in the Book of Revelation. This passage long has been associated with the Blessed Virgin, hence the crescent moon and stars in many paintings of Our Lady.

The **Cross Fitched,** with its spreading arms, is held to refer to the Word going out into the world.

Given to the Glory of God and in Honour of
Mr. & Mrs. William Walker Hinnant
and
Mr. & Mrs. Ernest Foster Thomas
by Mr. & Mrs. Michael David Mangum

I 0.

---

* In the Book of Numbers, the rod of Aaron budded forth **almonds,** signifying his priesthood. And legend says that the staff of Joseph blossomed and showed that he had God's divine favor when he was selected for Mary's husband.

** The monogram also represents **Miriam**—in Hebrew, meaning **star.**

The Palm Sunday liturgy is one of the most dramatic in the Church Year. It begins with the joyous acclamation of Christ's Triumphal Entry with its "Hosanna to the Son of David" then changes to the shouts of "Crucify him" in the reading (or traditional chanting) of the Passion Gospel, foretelling the events of Holy Week.

Jesus left Bethany (the House of Dates) to travel to Jerusalem. As He rode on a donkey, through the **stone gate** to His death, the people waved **palms** to praise the Son of David and shouted, "Blessed is he that cometh in the name of the Lord." This recognition of Christ's Lordship, as well as a prefiguring of His death, is shown in the initials **"INRI"** (the Latin abbreviation for "Jesus of Nazareth, King of the Jews"), which Pilate had placed on a placard in three languages on Christ's cross.

At the top of the window, the **Jerusalem Cross** is the traditional symbol of Jerusalem from at least the days of the Crusaders, where it appears in gold on a silver field in the Arms of the Crusader Kings of Jerusalem.*

*Given to the Glory of God and in Memory of
Hal Venable Worth, Jr. and Mary Simmons Andrews Worth
by Hal V. Worth III, Julia Worth Ray and
Holladay Worth Sanderson*

11.

---

* This Coat of Arms is striking because it breaks the rule in hearaldry that a metal cannot be placed on a metal. The combination of gold and silver was allowed because the Holy City itself is so remarkable. The combination of five crosses reminds us of the five wounds of Christ.

12.

The increasing gloom of Holy Week foreshadows the major events of the *"Triduum Sacrum,"* the three sacred days of Maundy Thursday, Good Friday, and Holy Saturday. The symbols for this Holy Week window are ones dealing with the preparations for those great events. The **money-bag and coins** refer to the thirty pieces of silver for which Judas betrayed Our Lord; the **lantern** alludes to the band of men preparing to arrest Our Lord in the Garden of Gethsemane after Judas' betrayal of Christ with a kiss. As the Passion according to St. John states, the band of men given Judas by the Chief Priests and Pharisees went to the Garden of Gethsemane "with lanterns and torches and weapons," pitting this world's little light against the Light of the World.*

At the bottom, the **thistle** represents sin and sorrow on earth, for God cursed the ground for Adam's sake. The **goldfinch**, which eats thorny plants, may thus symbolize the Passion that the "New Adam," Christ, suffered for the sins of Adam and his heirs.

Above, the **Tau Cross with a Serpent** is an excellent example of a symbol as being taken *in malo* (a symbol of evil) but actually being *in bono* (having a good meaning). Symbols are usually rich in significance, and often the same symbol stands for different things depending on its context. Here the serpent is not the Old Serpent Satan but Christ, for it refers to Moses' lifting up the Brazen Serpent to cure the snake-bitten Israelites in the Wilderness. The Brazen Serpent has thus become a type of Christ lifted up on the Cross to cure all mankind of their sins.

Given to the Glory of God and in Memory of
Roselle and Robert Watson and Annie and Frank Harward
by Samuel Robert Watson, Jr. and Lillian Harward Watson

---

* **Purple** adorns the windows of Holy Week as the seasonal color for penitence.

MAUNDY THURSDAY, THE HOLY EUCHARIST

Maundy Thursday is another liturgy of dramatic change, for it commemorates the sacrament of the Holy Eucharist at the beginning of Christ's Passion. Thus the festival white hangings of the Eucharist for this day are traditionally stripped off of the altar, leaving it bare for Good Friday.

The sacramental **bread and wine** of the Last Supper dominate both the day and this window.* Below the bread and wine is a **basin, ewer, and towel**, reminding us of Christ washing the feet of the disciples at the Last Supper. This example of Our Lord's love, humility, and service is still found frequently in the traditional foot-washing ritual of Maundy Thursday. One of the chants sung during this ceremony, *"Mandatum novum,"* gives us the day's name, "A new commandment give I unto you, that ye love one another."

The **grapes and wheat** rising from the bottom of the window remind us of the Holy Eucharist, while the pointed **Passion Cross** at the window's top prompts us to remember that we are at the beginning of Our Lord's Passion.

*Given to the Glory of God and for the Miracle Healing of
Betsy Anne Clendenin Bradshaw
Good Friday, April 8, 1977
by Mr. & Mrs. Charles W. Bradshaw, Jr.*

13.

---

* The day itself is so full of Christ's Passion that the medieval Church set aside the Thursday after Trinity Sunday as the Feast of the Body of Christ, Corpus Christi, to honor the Blessed Sacrament.

MAUNDY THURSDAY, THE DENIAL

After the Last Supper, the gloom again sets in. The increasing dolefulness of Holy Week was mirrored in the ancient ceremonies of *Matins and Lauds* for the last three days of Holy Week. These offices were called *"Tenebrae,"* (darkness), following the custom of gradually extinguishing candles during the service; it is the increasing darkness that we contemplate in this window.

After the Last Supper, Christ went out with his disciples across the brook Cedron to the Garden of Gethsemane. Here He went apart to pray: "O my Father, if it be possible, let this cup pass from me. Nevertheless, not as I will but as Thou wilt." This **Cup of Bitterness**, with the **Passion Cross**, is placed above a cock. The **cock** stands for Peter's own betrayal of Christ. After Judas and his band arrested Jesus, Peter followed behind. Discovered as one of Christ's disciples, Peter denied Christ three times before cockcrow, as Jesus had foretold. Peter went out and wept bitterly.

The bitterness of the **dandelion** makes it a suitable symbol of the Passion, and **Three Crosses** on a hillock speak of the coming Crucifixion of Our Lord, between two thieves, at Golgotha.

Given to the Glory of God and in Memory of
Elsie Lumsden Clendenin, September 1, 1959
and
James Ivan Clendenin, May 24, 1950
by Mr. & Mrs. Charles W. Bradshaw, Jr.

14.

From Maundy Thursday, we turn to the bare altar and **Passion red** or **black** of Good Friday. Everything pauses on Good Friday to reflect on Christ's Passion. The Church will not consecrate the Sacrifice of the Mass from Maundy Thursday until the Easter Vigil, preoccupied as she is with meditating on the historical Sacrifice of Christ on the Cross.

The bitterness of that Passion is suggested by the flowering **gall.** As the Psalmist says: "They gave me gall to eat: and when I was thirsty they gave me vinegar to drink." This foreshadows the gall offered Christ on the Cross. Above the gall is the **basin and ewer** with which Pontius Pilate, Roman Governor of Judea, symbolically washed his hands of the death of Christ. The **Crown of Thorns and Nails** refers to the mockery of the soldiers who crowned Christ with thorns, while the nails refer to Christ's Crucifixion. In Christian art, the Crown of Thorns is generally shown as a wreath, though it may have been a sort of cap.

The Latin Cross of the Crucifixion with **"INRI"** ("Jesus of Nazareth, King of the Jews") recalls Christ's Kingship, as Pilate had ordered the acronym displayed on the Cross.* The Cross itself here dominates the window and extends into the windows on either side, accentuating the events of Holy Week and of Easter. The Cross on which the salvation of the world depended thus bears witness to Our Lord's most bitter agony and death.

"Again, in spite of that, we call this Friday good."
(T. S. Eliot)

Given to the Glory of God
by Maurice N. Courie and Bobbi Otis Courie

15.

---

* Also written in Hebrew and in Greek.

EASTER SUNDAY

16.

The horror of the events of Holy Week suddenly turns from the darkness that covered the earth to Easter **white** in the change from Lenten shadows to Paschal light, "the light of Christ." The Cross which on Friday was the instrument of cruel death is now seen as the symbol of eternal life:

> Faithful Cross, above all other,
> one and only noble Tree:
> none in foliage, none in blossom,
> none in fruit thy peer may be.
> Sweetest wood, and sweetest iron,
> sweetest weight is hung on thee.

This hymn by Fortunatus, used in the ancient Good Friday liturgy, glorifies the Cross because that "sweetest weight" of Our Lord's Body was not held by death but rose again.

Thus the **Celtic Cross in Glory** eminates rays of splendor, praise, honor and radiance from a circle symbolizing eternity.

Below the Cross is the triumphant **Agnus Dei** Who has taken away the sins of the world; here we have not only the Sacrificial Lamb of God, but the Lamb of God bearing the banner of Victory Over Death. The uncommon position of this Triumphant Lamb's head is a reminder of Jesus' unnatural birth and His unnatural death and resurrection.

The **stream of four colors** suggests the River of Life, hinting also at the four rivers of the earthly paradise of Eden.* They also make us aware of the water of Holy Baptism.**

At the bottom, the **butterfly**, a common symbol of resurrection, and the **pomegranate** complete the scheme. The pomegranate refers not only to Christ's Resurrection but to His Church, for its many seeds make up one body.

Given to the Glory of God and in Memory of
Katherine Spellman Sawyer, 1901 - 1986
by Isaac Vaughn Manly and Peggy Sawyer Manly

---

* The four rivers of the Gospels (Matthew, Mark, Luke and John): Tigris, Pison, Gihon and Euphrates.
** The placement of the church's font between this window and the Good Friday window recalls spiritual rebirth from death and sin to eternal life. The early church held Baptisms at Easter, and this tradition is still found in the rite of Easter Vigil.

THE ASCENSION

"God has gone up with a merry noise, and the Lord with the sound of the trump. Alleluia." The Ascension of Our Lord is indicated by the soaring eagle, whose rising suggests also the Resurrection of Our Lord.

The Bestiary tradition associated with the **eagle** held that the eagle renewed his youth by flying up near the sun, then plunging to dip himself three times in a fountain. This has come to signify spiritual regeneration. The eagle is also the symbol of St. John the Evangelist, an attribution derived from the four "living creatures" of Ezekiel's vision. Here, however, the eagle is Christ, for supposedly the eagle can look directly at the blazing sun, perhaps as the Son can turn His eyes to the Father.

The **clouds** recall the clouds which hid Our Lord from sight at the Ascension. As the angels told the disciples, "Ye men of Galilee, why stand ye gazing up into heaven: in like manner as ye have seen him go into heaven so shall he come again."

Above, the **"Chi Rho"** monogram for Christ is surrounded by an acrostic: the Greek letters for "icthus," or "fish," which stand for the first letters in the Greek phrase "Jesus Christ, God's Son, Savior." It was this phrase that led to the Christian's early adoption of the fish as a sign of the Faith.

The **Chariot of Fire** in which Elijah ascended to heaven prefigures Christ's Ascension.

Below, the **acacia** symbolizes the immortality of the soul. The burning bush (aflame but not consumed) experienced by Moses and related in Exodus 3:1-6 is said to have been an acacia.

Given to the Glory of God and in Thanksgiving for His Many Blessings by Barbara and Hayne Palmour III

17.

PENTECOST, THE COMING OF THE HOLY GHOST

Sanctus
Spiritus

The festival white which has expressed the joy of the Easter season is replaced with red on Pentecost, though this is not Martyrs' red but rather the **joyful red** of the fire of the Holy Ghost. The tongues of fire which came on the apostles at Pentecost thus color all our meditations on the work of the Holy Ghost.

Pentecost comes the seventh week after Easter.

Above the flames, **seven doves** represent the seven gifts of the Holy Ghost: wisdom, understanding, counsel, fortitude, knowledge, godliness, and fear of the Lord. The dove itself is symbolic of the Holy Ghost, **Sanctus Spiritus**, for the Holy Ghost appeared in that form at Christ's Baptism.

The theme of the seven gifts of the Holy Ghost is further carried out with the **columbine plant**, which has seven petals or a seven-blossomed stalk.

The **triparted Cross Fleurée** here reminds us that the Holy Ghost is of one substance with the Holy and Undivided Trinity. It is for this reason that the Feast of the Holy Ghost is second in importance only to Easter: with Christmas and Easter, it is one of the three great Feasts of the Christian year.

Given to the Glory of God and in Memory of
Irish Lillian Howsam, 1893 - 1970
by Mr. & Mrs. Peter Somerville Howsam

18.

PENTECOST, THE BEGINNING OF THE CHURCH

Another aspect of the Feast of Pentecost, along with the Descent of the Holy Ghost, is that it is the beginning of the Church. The **beehive,** which St. Ambrose used as a comparison to the Church, with the bees as Christians working within it, stands for the Church.

The **fish** recalls the Church's early symbol for The Lord, and the acrostic, in Greek letters, represents the words: "Jesus Christ, God's Son, Savior."

A **mustard plant** symbolizes the faith of the Church, for Our Lord used the mustard seed as an indication of what little faith is needed even to move mountains. From the tiny seed grows a large plant with multiple usage.

Surrounding the **Greek Cross** is another Greek monogram: "Jesus Christ, Conqueror." Where there are curved marks above the letters, it means that the letters are an abbreviation.

Given to the Glory of God and in Thanksgiving for His Many Blessings by Mr. & Mrs. Bryce Wagoner

19.

TRINITY SUNDAY

The Octave (or eighth day of a major feast) of Pentecost came in the Middle Ages to be the Feast of the Trinity. Thus the red of Pentecost changes to the **white** of Trinity Sunday.

This Feast, most unusual in honoring a doctrine* rather than a person or an event, was popular in England, partly through its association with St. Thomas Becket, the martyred Archbishop of Canterbury, who was consecrated on this day. In the good old days, the following Sundays were "Sundays after Trinity"; now the 1979 *Book of Common Prayer* follows the custom of dating from the older Feast with "Sundays after Pentecost."

The "**Coat of Arms of the Faith**" in the middle of the window illustrates the essence of the mystery of the Trinity with its symbolism: "The Father is not the Son is not the Holy Ghost; the Father is God, the Son is God, the Holy Ghost is God." This symbol is thus a visual working out of definitions in the Athanasian Creed, which itself grew out of the formulations of the Councils of Nicaea and Constantinople in the fourth century.

In keeping with symbols of the Trinity, and the relation of Christ to the Trinity, a **Cross Fleurée** is placed in a Triangle. The three-leaved **shamrock** has long been a Trinitarian symbol, for its three leaves are joined as one. And the **acanthus,** a very hardy plant, suggests the eternal nature of the Triune God. Acanthus leaves are depicted at the top of many Greek columns.

20.

Given to the Glory of God and in Thanksgiving for Our Children
David James Coleman III and Nancy Berkeley Coleman Talley
by D. James Coleman, Jr. and Maydwelle Mason Coleman

---

* The doctrine of the Holy and Undivided Trinity is, strictly speaking, a mystery; that is, the doctrine is not contrary to reason but cannot be fully understood by reason, and that the truth of the doctrine is revealed rather than demonstrated.

The season we now enter is sometimes called "Ordinary Time"; it is devoted more to the Church's life than it is to the major commemorations of Our Lord's Life, and it occupies the longest sections of the Church Year, some two dozen Sundays or so, depending on the date of Easter. From Trinity Sunday to the First Sunday in Advent, the **green** hangings of the "Sundays after Pentecost" remain largely undisturbed except for Saints' Days and the Feast of the Transfiguration of Our Lord. The latter Feast is also remembered in the lessons of the Sunday just before Lent.

The season of Sundays after Pentecost (meaning fiftieth day) gives the Church time to reflect on her mission and the Christian Life. This window, the first of three for this season, exhibits a **scroll** for church membership, recalling the only true Church roll, The Book of Life. The **Lamp of Wisdom** recalls the old Introit for the Fourth Sunday after Trinity, "Dominus illuminatio mea": "The Lord is my light, and my salvation, whom then shall I fear?"

The **plantain** is used in Renaissance art to suggest the well-trodden path of the Faithful to Christ, presumably because the plant grew along roads or paths. The **Anchor Cross** symbolizes Christ as our hope. In the catacombs, the anchor was used as a symbol of hope and steadfastness, for St. Paul refers to hope as the anchor of the soul.

Given to the Glory of God and in Memory of
Anna C. and Harold L. Wright
by Mr. & Mrs. John N. Wright

2 1.

SUNDAYS AFTER PENTECOST (2)

2 2.

The Church's worship is the theme of this window. The **bells** give a joyful summons to worship, perhaps with the change-ringing so beloved by our Anglican ancestors and still heard Sunday morning in many English towns. The **open Bible**, the Word of God, indicates not only the lessons read in church but also the study of Holy Scripture commended of all Christians.

Yet both symbols suggest warning, for Scripture warns us to flee from evil and bells warn us of evil at hand. The old Offertory for the Mass of the Fifth Sunday after Trinity, "Exaudi Domine," expressed this idea: "I will thank the Lord for giving me warning: I have set God always before me: for he is on my right hand, therefore I shall not fall."

The **bulrush** recalls God's providence for his people in saving the infant Moses found in the bulrushes. The bulrush grows by water, and thus is sometimes thought to represent those who abide by the teachings of the Church, itself the stream for Living Water.*

The **Calvary, or Graded, Cross** is raised on three steps or "degrees," possibly indicating the Theological Virtues of Faith, Hope, and Charity, which are the virtues that St. Paul relates in I Cor. 13:13—"For now abidith faith, hope, charity, these three; but the greatest of these is charity."

Given to the Glory of God and in Memory of Twins
Ben Dixon, May 29, 1869 - September 29, 1918
and
Wright Dixon, May 29, 1869 - October 22, 1955
by Prince and Wright Dixon

---

* Job 8:11—"Can the rush grow up without mire? Can the flag grow without water?"

his window, focusing on two major Feasts in the season as well as the Sundays which fall in this season, recalls the ancient Offertory used in the Mass for the Ninth Sunday after Trinity: "The statutes of the Lord are right, and rejoice the heart, sweeter also than honey, and the honeycomb: and moreover the servant keepeth them." The **honeycomb** further suggests the Church's Lord, Who is sweeter than honey, an analogy aided by the association of Christ with the Bridegroom in the Song of Songs, whose lips drip honey.

The **Sun of Righteousness** is another Old Testament term applied to Our Lord from the Book of the Prophet Malachi. Here the Sun bears the monogram **"IHC,"** a variant of the first letters of "Jesus" in Greek. This symbol may bring to mind the Feast of the Transfiguration of Our Lord, at which He appeared to SS. Peter, James, and John in brilliant raiment with His face shining "as the sun." This manifestation of Christ's glory, recalled in the lessons of the Last Sunday after the Epiphany set in the 1979 *Book of Common Prayer*, is kept on the sixth of August. Not only the glory of the Church's Lord but also His love for the Church is found in this window.

Myrtle was in ancient times associated with love, and here it stands for the love of Christ's followers for the Lord Who first loved them.

The **Tau Cross**, or "T" cross, was a form of cross commonly used in Roman times for executions. It likewise is suggestive of the first letter of the Greek "Theos," or "God," when written in the Latin alphabet.* The Cross reminds us of Holy Cross Day, kept on 14th September.

*Given to the Glory of God
by Mr. & Mrs. Robert C. Greene*

23.

---

* In Greek, the first letter of "Theos" is a theta, which looks like a zero with a horizontal bar.

MICHAELMAS

24.

The Feast of St. Michael and All Angels is of particular importance to any church in the dedication of the Archangel. Popular devotion to angels and to St. Michael was widespread in the Middle Ages; witness the fame of Mont-Saint-Michel in France. Furthermore, St. Michael gave his name to a premier order of French chivalry. In those days the Archangels mentioned in Scripture, SS. Michael and Gabriel (including St. Raphael, named in the Book of Tobit, and the Holy Guardian Angels) all had separate feasts. Traditionally, the Anglican Communion remembers all Angels on the Feast of St. Michael on September 29.

The **scales** in the upper part of the window recall St. Michael's ascribed actions, at the Judgement, of weighing souls and of guiding them to God after death, a tradition kept alive until recent times in the Offertory of the Requiem Mass and in the lovely Celtic prayers and invocations to St. Michael.

St. Michael's role as the heavenly warrior who conquers the dragon in the Book of Revelation is also remembered here by his **sword** and by the **wounded dragon**, Satan.

In the upper part of the window, we have a **shield** alluding to St. Paul's shield of Faith, bearing a red Cross of Christian zeal.*

The **Michaelmas Daisy**, at the bottom of the window, blooms around Michaelmas Day, September 29th, hence its name.

Given to the Glory of God and in Honour of
The Rev. Lawrence Kemster Brown
by Anonymous Donors

---

* St. George, the patron Saint of England, also a dragon-slayer, is historically shown with a similar shield, silver with Cross "throughout," i.e., to the shield's edges. This red cross on white field (for silver), depicted here, is the flag flown by parish churches in England.

All Saints Day, itself a **white** day like Michaelmas, actually commemorates all saints and martyrs. During the Church year, the Church observes both Greater and Lesser Saints' Days as well, using **white** for "confessors" and the like who were not martyred, and **dark red** for the martyrs.

It is with the martyrs that the cult of the Saints began. The **red roses** for their blood and the **white lilies** of purity make up the wreath of eternal life at the bottom of the window.

Above the wreath, a **censer** with burning incense recalls the ancient idea of the prayers of the Saints arising to God, while the **"Hand of God"** suggests to us that His Providence is always over His Saints.

The **True Vine** (Christ) in which the Saints abide is combined with **four doves**, here symbolic of the souls of the Saints or of the Faithful Departed who live in Christ. Perhaps the number of four might imply the Four Last Things "ever to be remembered," but which the Saints never forgot: heaven, hell, judgement and death.

The **Cross Flamant** connotes the ardor of the Saints, whose zeal for the House of the Lord consumed them. Likewise, the flames remind us of the Holy Spirit at Pentecost.

Given to the Glory of God and in Thanksgiving for
Col. Michael H. and Alice W. Austell
and
Roy S. and Anna Holly Dearstyne
by Catherine Austell Dearstyne

25.

CHRIST THE KING

26.

The Sunday next before Advent has many connotations. It used to be called "Stir Up Sunday" from the old Prayer Book Collect for that day: "Stir up, we beseech thee, O Lord, the wills of thy faithful people." In this Century, the Roman Church designated this Sunday as the Feast of Christ the King. This use, though not required by the 1979 *Book of Common Prayer*, has nonetheless had popular appeal in many Anglican churches as well.

The Kingship of Christ is a particularly appropriate theme for the last window of the series within the nave, for it emphasizes Christ's Heavenly Kingdom and its peace. At the end of the Church Year, Christ the King also reminds us of His Lordship over time, and of the Apocalypse. For the Church Militant (the living), the Church Year will begin again with another Advent. For the Church Triumphant (beyond time), the Reign of Christ is already made manifest.

Beneath the symbols of Kingship, the **sceptre** or staff and the **crown** (common to earthly monarchs), is a **laurel plant**, about which St. Paul reminds us that victor's wreaths were made. Its leaves are said not to wilt, which implies eternity and thus Christ's eternal reign.

The **Cross Triumphant**, the **orb** surmounted by a **cross**, shows Our Lord's dominion even over earthly kings, who themselves may tacitly acknowledge this by holding such an orb.*

Given to the Glory of God and in Memory of
Dolphus Taylor Fisher
July 25, 1916 - August 29, 1984
by Jean Grantham Fisher

---

* H. M. Queen Elizabeth II did so at her Coronation, following the ancient rites that go back to St. Dunstan a thousand years ago.

ST. MICHAEL'S PARISH WINDOW

NARTHEX WINDOW (A)

Upon entering the church, one sees on the right in the narthex a window bearing the **Seal of St. Michael's Church**, Raleigh. The Seal* indicates that St. Michael's Episcopal Mission was dedicated on April 15, 1950.**

Through faith in the Bible and in communion with Christ, members of Christ Episcopal Church (represented by the **weather vane**) and The Church of the Good Shepherd (depicted by the **Lamb**) joined together to establish St. Michael's.

The **ship** is representative of the Church itself and of the colonists who came to America seeking religious freedom. The **crozier** (or shepherd's crook) that extends through the center denotes that the Bishop is the recognized head of the organized Episcopal Church. It also reminds us that God is the shepherd of us all.

In the center is the **Pommée Cross**, associated with St. Michael for centuries, and the **scales** which recall, in Revelation, St. Michael as being the weigher of souls at the Last Judgement.

The Greek Cross, with its four equal arms, suggests equality in Christ, while the **cherry** represents the fruit of good works and the sweetness of character which arises from them.

Given to the Glory of God and in Memory of
Frank Holden Richards
March 25, 1940 - September 5, 1985
by Mrs. Frank Holden Richards, Mr. & Mrs. Stephen Francis Techet
and Mr. & Mrs. Edward Nelson Richards

27.

---

* The St. Michael's Seal was designed by the Rev. Douglas E. Remer and Jay Cardy.
** It became a full parish the following year.

DIOCESAN WINDOW

28.

NARTHEX WINDOW (B)

The window on the left in the narthex bears the **seal of the Diocese of North Carolina**, of which this church is a part.*

The **ship** and its seven settlers recall those who came from England** to this first English colony in what would become the United States. The ship itself is traditionally a "type" of the Church, hearkening back to Noah's Ark and the remnant of those who were saved. The **twelve waves** are enhanced by four different shades of blue, alluding to the **four rivers** of the Gospels: Gihon, Tigris, Euphrates and Pison.

In the Seal are a **mitre and fanons+** bound by two **"Keys of the Kingdom"** which symbolize Absolution (left) and Excommunication (right), the latter being divided into seven segments for the seven deadly sins.

At the top of the window are the **Arms of the Episcopal Church in the United States**. The English Cross of St. George is differenced in the first quarter with a St. Andrew's Cross of stars on a blue field, thus paying allegiance to the Episcopal Church's British origins. **White** is representative of purity (God) and **red** symbolizes the blood of Christ.

The window alludes to the wholeness of the Church Universal: like the **willow**, it continues to grow as its branches are broken or pruned.

Given to the Glory of God and in Honour of
John A. Park, Jr.
First Mission Senior Warden - 1950
First Church Senior Warden - 1951
by S. Leigh Park and Bruce R. Park

---

* A Diocese identifies the district over which a Bishop has authority.
** Hence the Cross of St. George flying from the mast.
+ Worn by the Bishop, a mitre is a headpiece with two folds of cloth (fanons) attached to the back, representing the Spirit and the Letter of the Testaments.

Chronological History
of the Nave Windows

July 19, 1982 — St. Michael's Vestry approved the organization of a committee to research stained glass windows for the church.

August 31, 1982 — First meeting of the stained glass window committee was held.

January 31, 1985 — The vestry, with the approval of the architectural committee, accepted the concept of a design by The Willet Stained Glass Studios in Philadelphia, and approved the choice of Willet's to fabricate the windows. The vestry also directed the window committee to include the chapel and narthex windows in the full project.

April 15, 1985 — The concept of relating the liturgical story in an orderly sequence, Mary Patricia Stumpf's design concept as presented, and permission to contract the 28 windows were approved by the vestry.

May 19, 1986 — Designs for the 28 windows were approved.

September 8, 1986 — Twelve pledges were received for the first windows.

December 1986 — Three windows were installed.

December 25, 1986 — All 28 nave windows and the chapel window were subscribed.

May 31, 1987 — Installation of the 28 nave windows was completed.

June 7, 1987 — A Choral Eucharist and dedication of the windows took place at the 10:00 A.M. service.

History of the Chapel Window

With the placement of the chapel window, one might find an interruption of the liturgy as depicted in the nave windows; however, an effort was made by the artist, Mary Patricia Stumpf, to incorporate a consistent circulation and yet retain an emphasis on the services that occur in the chapel.

The transparency of the design was intentional so that the window could allow the worship from the chapel to be incorporated into the meditative beauty of the garden adjacent to the chapel.

The Willet Stained Glass Studios specially engineered the frame of the window to accommodate the vine of life throughout and yet to give support for the large pieces of glass.

On July 20, 1987, St. Michael's Vestry approved the design of the chapel window. Gifts for the funding of the window were received, and installation was completed May 20, 1988. During the 8:00 A.M. service on May 29, 1988, "The Window of the Holy Spirit" was dedicated.

Joy Batchelor

Chapel Window
THE WINDOW OF THE HOLY SPIRIT

In our chapel, we experience, through worship and meditation, the rites and sacraments of our Christian faith. "The Window of the Holy Spirit" can be interpreted to reiterate the love, devotion and praise that we feel and proclaim during these ceremonies.

The integral weaving of the **vine** reminds us of John 15:5: "I am the vine, ye are the branches: He that abideth in me, and I in him, the same bringeth forth much fruit: for without me ye can do nothing."

From this Vine, we receive the bread and wine (**wheat and grapes**) of the Eucharist.

We remember the **dove** as representing the Holy Spirit. In the Vine, we are joined in Holy Matrimony (two doves); through the Vine, we experience Pentecost and the seven gifts of the Holy Spirit (seven doves); in Baptism, we are regenerated by the Holy Spirit (a descending dove), and in death, we are surrounded by the Vine of eternal life—through the Father, through the Son, through the Holy Spirit, three-in-one.

A **chapel** is a Christian setting of worship, a sanctuary, a "place of refuge." By the very design of St. Michael's Chapel, we feel a sense of God's Light flowing in and out through the window, surrounding us with comfort and strength. A chapel is a place to praise God and to rejoice, a sanctuary in which to experience peace and tranquillity. Just as a **garden** can offer a place for worship and meditation, it is appropriate that our garden and our chapel are adjacent to each other and that they both afford refuge and celebration.

All of the above are symbols of "an outward and visible sign of an inward and spiritual grace." They are gifts given in loving memory and in honour of those whom we wish to remember, who have been symbols for us during our life on earth.

The Window of the Holy Spirit **has been given:**

To the Glory of God and In Loving Memory of
Zack B. Starritt, (1924 - 1986)
*by Helen Starritt, Richard and Judy Starritt, Jonathan Starritt,
and Heather Starritt*

To the Glory of God and in Loving Memory of
Our Parents and Grandparents
Ellen Elizabeth Howell Davis (1891 - 1932),
Orrin Leonard Davis (1888 - 1959),
Ruth Luena Wicks Quin (1903 - 1986),
William Richard Quin (1898 - 1972)
*by Dr. and Mrs. James Howell Davis, William Richard Quin Davis, Jonathan Orrin Quin Davis,
Charles Benjamin Quin Davis, Elizabeth Ruth Quin Davis, and James Howell Quin Davis*

(continued)

To the Glory of God and In Honour of
Our Children and Grandchildren
Sarah and John Hartpence,
Cynthia and Scott Knight,
Bobbi Hartpence Forbis,
Charlyne Jeanette Hartpence,
Kenneth John Hartpence,
Cynthia Elizabeth Knight,
Thompson Scott Knight, Jr.,
and sister, Elizabeth Thompson Gauss
by Kenneth T. and Clara T. Knight

To the Glory of God and In Honour of
The Richard Gibran Saleeby, Sr. Family

The Window of the Holy Spirit was dedicated on May 29, 1988.

The Chapel has been given:
To the Glory of God and In Loving Memory of
The Reverend Aldert Smedes (1810 - 1877)
and
The Reverend Bennett Smedes (1837 - 1899)
by James M. Poyner and Mary Poyner York

The Garden, which reflects God's beauty, peace and love,
has been given:
To the Glory of God
by Dr. and Mrs. Isaac A. Manly

The Manly Garden was dedicated in 1970.

History of the Angel Window

The late Thomas A Fraser, Jr., Bishop of the Diocese of North Carolina, suggested to Mary Patricia Stumpf, artist/designer, that the "Twenty Third Psalm" would be an appropriate theme for the narthex window. With great deliberation, Ms. Stumpf contacted various religious denominations, and even Pope John Paul II, to obtain diverse viewpoints and to absorb the spiritual quality generated by this familiar psalm.

The result of her prayerful, exhaustive inquiries was presented to the stained glass window committee on November 12, 1988. After acceptance by the committee, and by the architectural committee on January 28, 1988, the vestry gave full approval of her rendering at its March 21, 1988, meeting.

Sufficient funds were collected by August 18, 1990, for the vestry to approve installation of the upper triangle portion of the window. In February 1991, that segment was completed.

After the Rev. Dr. Charles M. Riddle III became the interim rector of St. Michael's Church in 1995, interest in completing "The Angel Window" soared, and with the enthusiasm of the vestry and parishioners, the contract for the remaining portion was signed on June 11, 1996.

One year later, in July 1997, St. Michael's completed stained glass window project became a reality, and on October 26, 1997, a glorious service took place to dedicate all of the windows to souls who have gone before and to friends who remain on this earth. St. Michael's commemorates the art form that magnifies the Light of God with the refraction of light through colored glass. It enhances worship. It is spiritual. Thanks be to God!

Please see illustration of the Angel Window on back cover.

THE ANGEL WINDOW

Artist/designer Mary Patricia Stumpf was inspired through reflection on the many passages from the Bible that paraphrase, reiterate and reinforce the "Twenty Third Psalm."* This text for the narthex window was suggested by the late Thomas A. Fraser, Jr., Bishop of the Diocese of North Carolina.

"Psalms . . . provide insight into the devotional life of the people who first used them. Their real feelings find utterance here, feelings of grief and joy, of despair and hope, of anger and penitence, of passionate entreaty for help or calm assurance of trust."**

Initially, Ms. Stumpf made two observations. One was of the simple statement about our church that was voiced by the architect, Leif Valand, "The building should be so constructed that when you enter into it, you wish to kneel down and say a prayer." The other consideration was that the narthex window "....should be a summation of the expression of faith at St. Michael's; that the window should tell of the eternal, not the transitory, qualities of its subject. It should speak not of flesh and blood, but of the spirit of mankind and the Holy Spirit of God."

Angelic beings remind one of numerous references in the Bible to angels as intercessors between God and human beings: the birth of John, the Annunciation, the Nativity, shepherds, the massacre of the Holy Innocents, the Resurrection. Here they are depicted as moving freely between the Trinity and humankind's earthly existence.

The top portion of the window depicts the triune God: three crosses maintaining one, symbolic of the **Trinity;** the rays of **Glory** (praise, splendor and honor) radiating from God, and the **unending circle**, representing life eternal.

The rendering of the **landscape** reminds one of the earthly existence of humankind.

Because of the two flowing angels that dominate the window, parishioners at St. Michael's began to refer to the window as "The Angel Window." The depiction often brings images of a very personal nature to observers and heightens one's sensitivities to the familiar words of the "Twenty Third Psalm."

---

* i.e., Psalms 16 and 91; Isaiah 43 and 44; Mark 1:13, etc.

** *Kerygma Resource Book* by James A. Walther

DONORS AND DONEES OF THE ANGEL WINDOW
To the Glory of God

In Loving Memory of:

Robert Mayne & Frances Albright

Crayne & Snowden Albright Howes
Mr. & Mrs. Charles Blanchard
Mr. & Mrs. Micou F. Browne
Frank & Mary Euwer Crawley
Mr. & Mrs. Oliver Crawley
Mrs. Jean G. Fisher
Mr. & Mrs. W. Harris Grimsley
Mr. & Mrs. Peter Howsam
Martha B. Kahdy
Mr. & Mrs. Frank R. Kennedy, Jr.
Billie S. Little
Mr. & Mrs. Daniel S. Little
Dr. & Mrs. Frank Longino
North Carolina Beer & Wine Wholesale Co.
Mr. & Mrs. Winston Page, Jr.
Christine H. Rankin
Nettie H. Reid
Mrs. S. N. Smith
Mary McCue Webb
Mr. & Mrs. F. Carter Williams
Colvin M. Worth
Sara B. Wright

William H. Aldridge, Jr.

Mr. & Mrs. Burke Haywood

Oliver Anderson

St. Michael's Episcopal Church Choir

Rear Admiral W. H. Ashford, Jr.

Mr. & Mrs. Wright Dixon, Jr.

H. Emerson Atkinson

Mr. & Mrs. James Black III

The Rev. James Dunbar Beckwith

Mr. & Mrs. Wright Dixon, Jr.
Mr. & Mrs. James A. Hill, Jr.

The Rev. Alfred R. and Sarah Bernard Berkeley Lawrence Eley and Anna Neal Blanchard

Charles F. & Bernard Berkeley Blanchard

James M. and Arbelia B. Boyette

James M., Jr. & Nancy Adams Boyette

David James Coleman, Jr.

May Coleman Grimsley
David James Coleman III
Nancy Coleman Talley
Mr. & Mrs. George Axford
Mr. & Mrs. Gerald A. Barrett
Mr. & Mrs. Virgil Burney
Gertrude N. Carstarphen
Certified Limb Professionals
Roberta O. Clark
Dr. & Mrs. Maurice N. Courie
Mr. & Mrs. Giles E. Crowell, Jr.
Mrs. James E. deLoach
Mr. & Mrs. William P. Duff, Jr.
Dr. & Mrs. Jack Durant
Episcopal Church Women, Diocese of North Carolina
Mr. & Mrs. John Farmer
Mr. & Mrs. Melvin L. Finch, Jr.
Mrs. Jean G. Fisher
Mr. & Mrs. J. H. Gerber
Mrs. Marjorie M. Goodwin
Mr. & Mrs. Harris Grimsley
Mr. & Mrs. Harold G. Hall
Dr. & Mrs. Randolph Hall
Mrs. Mary V. Harris
Mr. & Mrs. Louis L. Holder
Mr. & Mrs. Luther C. Hodges
Mr. & Mrs. William B. Keener
Mrs. Hanna R. Kitchin
Kiwanis Club of Golden K

Mr. & Mrs. Fred G. Liady
Mr. & Mrs. Fred London
Mr. & Mrs. Richard M. McClain
Barbara McCray
Mr. & Mrs. T. Kinlock Mahone
Mr. & Mrs. George Margeson
Mr. & Mrs. W. Forrest Matthews, Jr.
Mr. & Mrs. John R. Otto
Mr. & Mrs. Walter Pearson
Pinewood Garden Club
Mrs. Edwin C. Rochelle
Mr. & Mrs. Gus G. Saparillas
Easterbelle B. Sims
Mr. & Mrs. John Smith
Mr. & Mrs. Keith W. Smith
Mr. & Mrs. Nat Smith
Ms. Betty B. Stansel
Mr. & Mrs. William T. Stevens
Mr. & Mrs. James Tommerdahl
Mrs. Wymene Valand
Waddell Lodge #228 A.F. & A.M.
Evelyn T. Warburton
Mr. & Mrs. Van Wyck Webb
Mr. & Mrs. John W. Yowell, Jr.

Rosemary R. Cooke
Thomas Mial & Lisa Cooke Williamson

R. Oliver Crawley
Adelaide Winslow Crawley & their
    children:
    Martha Crawley Gallop
    Frank Winslow Crawley
    R. Oliver Crawley, Jr.
R. Mayne Albright
Kitty K. Anderson
Mr. & Mrs. Fred Armstrong
Caroline B. Bryan
Frances Buchanan
Alice T. Carson
Mrs. H. Royster Chamblee
William & Susan Cherry
Chestnut Grove Methodit Church
Marjorie M. Cullipher
Margaret Downes

Mr. & Mrs. G. D. Dusenbury
Mrs. Jean G. Fisher
Tom Fisher / Custom Brick
Mrs. M. Aubrey Gallop, Sr.
Mrs. E. Wood Gauss
J. W. Gordon
Mr. & Mrs. W. Harris Grimsley
Mr. & Mrs. Harold Hall
Mr. & Mrs. Henry Haywood
Mrs. Edward Jenkins
Mr. & Mrs. John R. Kernan
Frank & Betsy King
Kiwanis Golden K of Raleigh
Mr. & Mrs. Kenneth T. Knight
Mr. & Mrs. Wade Lewis, Jr.
Mr. & Mrs. Fred W. London
Mr. & Mrs. Rex Mann
Dr. & Mrs. Isaac Manly
Mrs. Phyllis Margeson
Mrs. J. L. Moore
Mr. & Mrs. Marvin Newsom
Bruce & Abbie Penwell
Charles A. Poe
Mrs. Edwin Rochelle
Frances Ricker Rowe
Ruth P. Saint Amand
Faye Senter
Mrs. Gordon Smith, Jr.
John Clayton Smith
Mr. & Mrs. Andy Sparks
Mr. & Mrs. Chris Thompson
Mr. & Mrs. Frank Thornton & Family
Dr. & Mrs. Lewis Thorp
Frances Vann
Mrs. Phyllis Wall
Josephine Ward
Mr. & Mrs. John W. Watson, Jr.
Dr. & Mrs. Francis Winslow

Cady Currin
Kathleen F. Hogg

Clarence Vroegin and
Evelyn Kreim Dewey
Susan Dewey Montgomery & Family

Rosa D. Duboise
Mr. & Mrs. Dale Stumpf

William Powell Duff, Jr.
Elizabeth Scott Duff
Claire Duff Dodd
William Powell Duff III

Mary Jane Dunn
Mrs. Adlaide Crawley
Martha & Marshall Gallop

Mary Matherly Durant
Jack Davis & Judy Johnson Durant

Minta Banks Eure
Armecia Eure Black
Mr. & Mrs. Lester E. Beesley
Mr. & Mrs. Don Coeyman
Mr. & Mrs. Wright Dixon, Jr.
Mrs. Robert S. Gaddis
Dr. & Mrs. Randolph Hall
J. Ollie Harris
Mrs. Claiborne Johnson
Elizabeth Johnston
Mrs. William Tall Jones
Nations Bank Commercial
Mr. & Mrs. Don Smith
Mrs. Phyllis Wall

Anne Sisk Farmer
Dr. & Mrs. Francis Winslow

The Rt. Rev. Thomas Augustus Fraser, Jr.
Marjorie Rimbach Fraser
Ted & Dorcas Bodenheimer
Dr. & Mrs. Garrett Briggs
Greg & Martha Crampton
Mr. & Mrs. Clarence Darling
Mrs. Betty Duff
Mr. & Mrs. Thomas Elliott
Mr. & Mrs. Melvin Finch, Jr.
Mr. & Mrs. William Gilliam
Lanny & Susanne Harer
Jim & Harriet Hill
Allen, Martin & Robert Hill
Mr. & Mrs. William Ingram

Mr. & Mrs. Walter Keezell
Priscilla Gilliam Laite
Mr. & Mrs. Tate Lanning
Mr. & Mrs. Richard McClain
Dr. & Mrs. Isaac Manly
Mr. & Mrs. Stan Meiburg
Mr. & Mrs. Richard M. Myers
C. A. Newcomb
Mr. & Mrs. William A. Pahl, Jr.
John A. Park, Jr.
Mr. & Mrs. Garland Radford
Dr. & Mrs. Richard Saleeby
Ms. Jane Stikeleather
Dale & Mary Patricia Stumpf
Mr. & Mrs. Banks Talley, Jr.
Mr. & Mrs. Henry Ward, Jr.
Mr. & Mrs. Hal Worth
Mr. & Mrs. Smedes York

Joan Gilmore
Dr. & Mrs. Isaac Manly

Irvin Givens
St. Michael's Senior Choir
Mr. & Mrs. Ben Booker

Grayson Rogers Givens
His parents

Benjamin Russell Harward
Eleanor Harward
Anonymous Donor
Mr. & Mrs. N. B. Banks
Mr. & Mrs. Gregory Crampton
Mr. & Mrs. Charles Culpepper
Mr. & Mrs. Wright Dixon, Jr.
Dr. & Mrs. Jack Durant
St. Michael's Epsicopal Church Women Board
Ruth C. Fox
Mr. & Mrs. A. E. Gibson
Mr. & Mrs. Harold Hall
Mr. & Mrs. Joseph Johnson
Mr. & Mrs. Kenneth Knight
Mr. & Mrs. John Lemay
Mr. & Mrs. Fred London
Dr. & Mrs. Isaac Manly

Mrs. J. L. Moore
Jean L. Newton
Doris M. Nooe
Oakland Acres Association
Ellen Pafford
Margaret Pruitt
Sarah Raynor
Mrs. Phyllis Wall
Mrs. Lillian Watson

Robert Tomlinson Hill

James A., Jr. & Harriet Tomlinson Hill
James Allen Hill III
Charles Martin Hill
Mrs. James C. Adams
Billy & Frances Adams
Mr. & Mrs. James C. Adams II
Mr. & Mrs. William Aldridge
Beki & Haywood Alexander
Thomas W. H. & Mickie Alexander
Martha & Julie Anderson
Mrs. Mildred Anderson
Apex Lumer Company
Fred, Lynda, Sara & Leslie Atkins
George & Kathy Auman
Charles & Peggy Barham
Celeste Barnes
Hal, Earleen, Mary Jane & Kenan Barnes
Barr-Mullin, Inc.
Bill & Brenda Bateman
Mrs. Marie G. Belser
Mrs. Frances Mae Bennett
Dr. & Mrs. Robert Bingham
Branch & Jill Bissette
Mrs. Jacquelyn J. Bissette
Paul & Bettie C. Bissette
Jim & Marsha Blackburn
John & Eleanor Blackwell
Beth Blankenship
Esther Tomlinson Bogle
Linwood & Amelia Bond
Ben, Mardi, David & Keri Booker
The Rev. Blair Both
Gene & Pat Boyce
Sam & Dixie Boyce

Jim & Nancy Boyette
Curtis, Betsy, Josh & Curt Brewer
Garrett, Sue & Molly Briggs
Bright Hope Laurel United Methodist
  Church
The Rev. Larry Brown
Mrs. Louise Hill Bryan
Jim and Dee Bullock
David Butts
Richard & Anita Byrum
Larry & Laura Caison
Carrington & Walker
Vernon Cason
David & Mary Cates
Bill & Susan Cherry
Joe & Carolyn Cheshire
Steve, Janet, Stephen & John Chiavetta
Clint & Martha Clampitt
Norwood & Judy Clark
Harvey & Mary Breck Clayton
Jack & Betsy Coble
Mrs. May Coleman
Coley Forest Garden Club
Bob & Peggy Collins
Colonial Bank
Mo & Bobbi Courie
Greg, Martha, Beth, Louisa & Anna
  Crampton
Frank & Betty Cranor
Frank, Mary Snow, Frank & Missy Crawley
Pat Crumpler
Currin Brothers, Inc.
Jim & Jean Daniel
Dwight, Sandra, Ward & Quinn Davis
Joseph & Anne Davis
Earl, Betsy, Meg & Buddy Deal
Mrs. Helen Deal
Ralph & Jerrie Dearborn
Russell & Lynn Dement
Dement, Askew, Gammon & Salisbury
C. A. Denson
Wright & Prince Dixon
Dougher Construction Company
Tom, Kathy, Carrie & Laura Dow

Bill & Sally Duff
Jack & Judy Durant
Bob & Jo Ann Eaves
Mrs. Mae Murray Elkins
Nikki, Mary Ann, Shannon & Jonathan Ellerbe
Root, Sue, Ashley & Justin Edmonson
Bill, Meta, Margaret & Will Ellington
Envirotek, Inc.
St. Michael's Episcopal Church Women Board
Neil, Anne, Kelly & Amy Evans
Mrs. Vivian Farmer
Grady, Lynda, Mary Hampton & Trace Ferrell
Mel & Nell Finch
Mrs. Jean Fisher
Bummy & Jean Fleming
Harold & Katherine Forehand
Mary Dee Foster
The Foundry of the Shoals, Inc.
Ron & Linda Fowler
Mrs. Marge Fraser
Charles & Donna Frazelle
Mrs. Margaret Frost
Jim, Mary Susan & Molly Fulghum
Bill & Bobbie Furr
Charlie & Lucy Gaddy
Charlie & Nancy Gaddy
Becky Garren
Col. & Mrs. Ralph W. Girdner
Mrs. Marge Goodwin
Bob & Jo Greene
Robert, Glenda, Ashley & Phil Gruber
Harold & Ann Hall
Randy & Beth Hall
Al & Ann & Hamrick
Ivan & Tempie Hardesty
Jack, Frankie, & John Harrington
Gene, Ann, Ann Martin & Amy Harris
Herbert Harris
Virginia Oliver Harris
Jim & Anne Hart
Capt. & Mrs. John C. Haynie, Jr.

Mrs. Dorothea Heinrich
Jennifer Hoffman
Max & Dottie Hiatt
Mrs. Daphne R. Hill
Harvey & Tal Hinnant
Hodge, Steward & Co.
Jennifer Hoffman
Kathleen F. Hogg
John Holbrook
Tim Holbrook
Faye Holliman
Howard, From, Stallings & Hutson
Peter & Shirley Howsam
Mr. & Mrs. John K. Hoyt
Calvin & Marilyn Hudson
Eli & Helen Hykal
Bill & Jackie Jackson
Travis & Mary Jackson
Paul & Carol Johnson
Roddy & Linda Jones
Joe & Jane Jordan
Glenn & Janet Kelly
Mimi Keravuori
Charles J. Kerr
Becky King
Virginia B. Kingsley
John & Lou Knight
Ken & Tommy Knight
Tate & Michael Lanning
Charles & Louise Latimer
Mrs. Elsie B. Lawrence
Pete & Willard Lee
Charlie & Terry Lefort
Bob & Evelyn Lightfoot
Jon, Annette, Jonathan & Julianna Lindsey
Alex & Carolyn MacFadyen
Mac & Ann McDonald
Sam & Harriet McNairy
McNamara, Pipkin, Knott & Carruth
Mrs. Alan McRae
Larry & Clare Maddison
Larry & Shirley Mangum
Michael & Tal Mangum
Ike & Peggy Manly

Henry & Sara Jo Manning

Dick, Nina, Shauna & Grant March

Mrs. Phyllis Margeson

Jessica Marlow

Wayne & Marianne Marshall

Ward & Julia Marslender

Frederick & Vivian Martin

George & Jean Martin

Hamilton & Sally Martin

Jack & Joan Martin

Mrs. Shirley Martin

Walter Matthews

Frank, Mary & Lydia Meece

Mr. & Mrs. W. Guy Mendenhall

Mrs. Jean Mercer

Allen & Brenda Millar

Steve, Susan, Sarah & Laura Montgomery

Mrs. Betty Moore

Joe, Julie, Elizabeth, Katherine &
    Joe Forrest Moore

Joe Moore & Company

Pattie Moore

Fred & Jeannie Morelock

Charlie & Becky Morris

Hugh & Pansy Morton

Sam Moss

Bob & Nancy Moxley

Bruce, Mary Lou, Bret, Carrie & Susan
    Muller

Bob & Marty Munt

Marvin & Bobbie Musselwhite

Elizabeth Neese

Mark & Sandy Newell

Tim, Anita & Cullen Nichols

Gillie & Gwen Nicholson

Gilliam, Margaret & Catherine Nicholson

Robert Nielsen

Tom & Jane Norris

North Carolina Association of CPA's

Nancy B. Norwood

Mrs. June Nuessle

Jim, Nancy & Jamie Nutt

Winston & Sandy Page

Larkin, Alice, Jamie, Kevin, Chris,
    Allison & Catherine Pahl

Jamie Pahl Concert

Billy, Martha, Anna & Sara Beth Pahl

Hayne & Barbara Palmour

Gary, Laura, Blair & Gray Pendleton

Matt Person

Mike, Barbara & Grey Perkins

Bill & Ann Pleasants

Bob Pollard

Dr. & Mrs. Robert Pope

Henry, Martha, Elizabeth & Alex Pope

Bob & Virginia Price

Garland, Lee, Lisa & Kam Radford

RAO Enterprises, Inc.

Mrs. Ila Mae Raper

Lindsay & Virginia Reed

Dave & Mary Rendleman

Margaret Reynolds

Dan, Karen, Chris & Jon Rhem

Bill Robertson

Allison Rouse

Charles & Bettie Bagley Rowe

Richard & Doris Saleeby

Steve & Paula Saleeby, Aaron & Adam
    Maruer

Chuck & Mary Scarantino

Dan, Glenna & Aimee Sears

Jack & Bette Severin

Nanci, Tim & Ellen Smith

Pete & Jeanette Smith

Kent, Vanessa, Andrew & Patrick Smyth

Mr. & Mrs. William Solari

Kenneth & Betsy Sprunt

Pat Sprunt

John & Jane Stephens

Tim & Cathy Stewart

Jane Stikeleather

Jane & Jill Stokes

A. E. Strange, Jr.

Harvey & Joan Striplin

Student Tour & Travel (Holbrook)

Dale, Pat & Brice Stumpf

Clayton, Prissy, Shawn, Shannon &
    Will Stufflebeam

Banks, Louise and Mary Louise Talley

Ben & Lianda Taylor

Steve, Joan, Alexandra & Andrew Techet
Mildred Barnes Thompson
Russell & Sis Thompson
George & Carol Thornhill
Andy, Candace, Dana & Dan Tomlinson
Bob, Lavinia, Charlotte, Robert &
    David Tomlinson
Charles, Susanna & Allen Tomlinson
Mrs. Eloise Martin Tomlinson
Stephan & Lauren Tomlinson
Mr. & Mrs. James W. Truitt
Alex & Virginia Turner
Ted & Betsy Vaden
Conner & Nancy Vick
Mrs. Phyllis S. Wall
Bill & Beth Wallace
Joe & Lucy Ware
Bill, Gail, Lisa & Bryan Waters
Van Wyck & Anna Webb
Mike, Nancy & Michael Weddington
Jim & Janet Whited
Crosby & Gussie Willet
Bill & Doris Williams
Dorothy R. Williamson
Jay Womble
Earle & Jean Wood
Frannie Wood
Kevin Woodard
Leon , Bonnie, Molly & Ben Woodruff
Hal & Lynne Worth
Marguerite Worth
Hunter, Jackie, Cameron & Hunt Wyche
Smedes & Rosemary York

Eva White Hinnant

Harvey Jackson & Talmadge Thomas
    Hinnant
Dr. & Mrs. Thad Barringer
Mrs. Robert Beam
Mr. & Mrs. Sid Gulledge
Mr. & Mrs. F. B. Hart
Mr. & Mrs. Roger Holman
Mrs. Elva A. Kost
Mr. & Mrs. Fred London
Mr. & Mrs. Richard McClain

Dr. & Mrs. Isaac Manly
Mr. & Mrs. William W. Minton
Mr. & Mr. J. L. Moore
Mr. & Mrs. R. F. Ruffner
Betty B. Stansel
Thomas C. Trumbull
Van Webb, Jr./Dupree & Webb, Inc.
Mrs. Nancy Willard

William Walker Hinnant

Harvey Jackson & Talmadge Thomas
    Hinnant
Atlantic Tobacco Company
Mr. & Mrs. Robert P. Buchanan, Jr.
Dupree & Webb, Inc.
Mr. & Mrs. Robert Edwards
Mr. & Mrs. Fred B. Hart
Mrs. Estelle R. Hinnant
Mr. & Mrs. W. J. Hudons III
Mr. & Mrs. Fred London
Mr. & Mrs. Richard M. McClain
Mr. & Mrs. W. E. Mangum
Mr. & Mrs. William W. Minton, Jr.
Mr. & Mrs. Joseph L. Moore
Mr. & Mrs. John A. Park, Jr.
Mr. & Mrs. R. F. Ruffner
Mrs. Ruth W. Thomas
Mrs. Roger I. Wall

Preston E. Hodges and
Frances Berry Hodges Caviness
Francis R. and Kathleen M. Hogg

David Marshall & Marianne Hodges Hogg
Kathleen Frances Hogg

William P. Johnston

Elizabeth B. Johnston
Mr. & Mrs. T. F. Armstrong
H. V. Barnette
Armecia Eure Black
Dr. & Mrs. Charles Boland
Mr. & Mrs. John C. Broughton
Barbara W. Buchanan
W. G. Clark III
Mr. & Mrs. Fred A. Coe
Mr. & Mrs. Don Coeyman

Mrs. R. E. Coggsdale
Mrs. Oliver Crawley
Starke Dillard
Rosalee M. Duffy
Early Risers AA
Alice F. Eure
Mr. & Mrs. Thad Eure
Fairview Group
James S. Fauver
Mr. & Mrs. Robert S. Gaddis
Jim & Joyce Gibson
Mr. & Mrs. W. Harris Grimsley
Hayes Barton Group
Louise W. Johnson
Jeanette S. Jones
Mr. & Mrs. W. Allen Kindel, Jr.
Mr. & Mrs. Kenneth T. Knight
Ruby Lamb
Mr. & Mrs. Jon Charles Long
Dr. & Mrs. Isaac Manly
Mr. & Mrs. H. G. Maxwell
Mrs. J. L. Moore
Mrs. J. G. Poole, Sr.
Mr. & Mrs. James Poyner/Poyner
  Foundation
Mr. & Mrs. Richard Raymond
John Clayton Smith
Norwood & Mary Starling
Frances Vann
Mrs. Roger I. Wall

Kathleen Pickett Keezell
Walter B. Keezell, Jr. & Children
Mr. & Mrs. Kenneth A. Aldridge
Mr. & Mrs. Richard Andrews
Mr. & Mrs. William J. Bateman, Jr.
Dr. & Mrs. V. B. Bensen
Charlotte A. Berrey
Mrs. J. D. Berrey
Dr. & Mrs. Gerald Blake
Mr. & Mrs. Kenneth E. Blevins
Mr. & Mrs. Cecil C. Bost
Mr. & Mrs. Hoyt C. Bowman, Jr.
Mr. & Mrs. James M. Boyette
Branch Banking & Trust Company

The Rev. Lawrence K. Brown
Mr. & Mrs. John L. Bryan
Mrs. Decatur G. Browne
G. A. Callahan
Mr. & Mrs. W. R. Casteen
Mr. & Mrs. Norm Chambers
Danny Cockerham/Milo C. Cockerham,
  Inc.
Mr. & Mrs. Rodney Coleman, Jr.
Mrs. William Coleman
Mrs. Grace Cooke
Dr. & Mrs. Maurice N. Courie
Mr. & Mrs. R. Douglas Cowan
Dr. & Mrs. James S. Coxe III
Mr. & Mrs. Arthur Cooper
Kathryn M. Cooper
Mr. & Mrs. Paul Cooper
Mr. & Mrs. Frank Cranor
W. L. Crowe
Mr. & Mrs. Clarence R. Darling, Jr.
Mr. & Mrs. Wright Dixon, Jr.
Dr. & Mrs. Jack Durant
Mr. & Mrs. Harry H. Dutton, Sr.
Robert O. Evans
Dr. & Mrs. Ronald Edwards
Mr. & Mrs. E. M. Eiland
Mr. & Mrs. Mel Finch, Jr.
Mr. & Mrs. Nolan S.Finklen
Mrs. Jean G. Fisher
Mr. & Mrs. Sam P. Fletcher
Food Systems, Inc.
Mr. & Mrs. L. R. Fritsch
Polly Frye
Dr. & Mrs. Preston Gada, Kathryn & Will
Mr. & Mrs. W. R. Gentry
Mr. & Mrs. Robert C. Greene, Sr.
Mr. & Mrs. Archie P. Gupton
Mr. & Mrs. Harold Hall
Mr. & Mrs. Randolph Hall
Mr. & Mrs. John T. Hardin
Dr. & Mrs. Alexander Hathaway
Mr. & Mrs. Thomas G. Hamm
Mr. & Mrs. William R. Harrison
Mr. & Mrs. Thomas T. Hay

Anne S. Hill
Jim & Harriet Hill
Mr. & Mrs. Harvey J. Hinnant
Mrs. Cornelia S. Hopkins
Mr. & Mrs. Robert L. Horky
Mr. & Mrs. Peter Howsam
Mr. & Mrs. Carl Hunt
Mr. & Mrs. C. D. Jamison, Jr.
Karen K. Johnson
Mr. & Mrs. James B. Jones, Jr.
Stan Kant & Associates
Mrs. N. H. Keezell, Sr.
Nat Keezell, Jr.
Mr. & Mrs. Kenneth T. Knight
Mr. & Mrs. Marvin B. Koonce, Jr.
Mr. & Mrs. J. Tate Lanning, Jr.
Nadine Lohr
Mr. & Mrs. Fred London
Mr. & Mrs. Alex MacFadyen
Mr. & Mrs. Harold McAllister, Jr.
Mrs. Irene McGinnis
Mr. & Mrs. Laurence B. Maddison, Jr.
Dr. & Mrs. Isaac Manly
Mrs. Phyllis Margeson
Mr. & Mrs. Wayne Marshall
Mr. & Mrs. W. F. Matthews
Mrs. Jean Mercer
Milestone Restaurant & Plaza #51
L. Barron Mills, Jr.
LeRoy & Sue Mitchell
Mrs. Joseph L. Moore, Sr.
Mrs. Lillian N. Moore
Nettie M. Moore
Mr. & Mrs. Ronald L. Moore
Mr. & Mrs. Thomas W. Moore
Jamye, Lindsey, Hunter, Allison & Marc Moore
Mr. & Mrs. Spears Mullen
Mr. & Mrs. H. Gilliam Nicholson, Sr.
Mr. & Mrs. Tom Noffsinger
Nancy Lu Otto
PCS Management Corp.
Mr. & Mrs. Winston Page
Mr. & Mrs. William A. Pahl, Jr.
Mr. & Mrs. J. Larkin Pahl

Dr. & Mrs. Hayne Palmour
Norman S. Parrish
Elizabeth Andrews Pearson
Mr. & Mrs. G. W. Pleasants
Mr. & Mrs. William D. Poe
Allison, Jeanie, Ross & John Thomas Poe
Mr. & Mrs. William E. Price
Janet M. Proctor
Randy, Mabel & Bob Rabb
Mr. & Mrs. Garland Radford & Bob
Mr. & Mrs. Lindsay Reed
Marion A. Ruch
Sadlers Brothers Oil Company, Inc.
Dr. & Mrs. Richard G. Saleeby
Samuels, Inc.
Seyen Investments/United Pacific Board of Directors & Employees
Myrtle M. Simmons
Simms Enterprises
Col. & Mrs. Edward T. Smith
John Clayton Smith
Mr. & Mrs. William R. Stein, Jr.
Mrs. Paul Stuart
Mr. & Mrs. John C. Thompson
Mr. & Mrs. George Thornhill III, Tad & Cooper
Mr. & Mrs. James G. Umbarger
Mr. & Mrs. Val Valentine
Mr. & Mrs. Bryce Wagoner
Harry & Sallie Walker
Mrs. Roger I. Wall
Mr. & Mrs. Van Wyck Webb
Rita L. Williams
Mr. & Mrs. James L. Wilson
Mr. & Mrs. Earle S. Wood
Mr. & Mrs. Hal Worth III

John R. Kernan
Louise E. Kernan
Brookfield Center School Staff
Mr. & Mrs. Wright Dixon, Jr.
Elizabeth Gauss
May Coleman Grimsley
Dr. & Mrs. Randolph Hall
Mr. & Mrs. Sam Napolitano & Family

Mr. & Mrs. Michael Ohlson
Ruth F. Painter
Gene C. Smith
Mrs. Phyllis S. Wall
William H. Williams
Mrs. C. A. Wood

Frank and Ethel Kriem

Susan Dewey Montgomery & Family
Bible Study Group:
   Valerie Brown
   Martha Crampton
   Sue Edmonson
   Marjorie Fraser
   Jennie Haase
   Jane Henderson
   Harriet Hill
   Mary Lou Muller
   Marty Munt
   Margaret Nicholson
   Judy Spaziano
   Jackie Wyche

Fitzhugh Lee

Mr. & Mrs. Garland Radford

Richard M. McClain

Betsy Tingley McClain
Richard Marvin McClain, Jr.
Lutie McClain Rayhart
James Ross McClain
Mr. & Mrs. John L. Amburn
Mr. & Mrs. Frank B. Anderson
Mr. & Mrs. Richard S. Andrews
Mr. & Mrs. T. F. Armstrong
Association of Military Banks of America
H. V. Barnette
William & Gloria Baugham
Mrs. Dorothy R. Branham
The Rev. & Mrs. E. Guthrie Brown
The Rev. & Mrs. Larry Brown
Mrs. W. H. Buchanan
Earl & Ruby Burton
Bette B. Cadwallader
Gertrude T. Card
Cornelia Chesson

Mr. & Mrs. Garth Childress
Mr. & Mrs. David W. Cox
Oliver & Adelaide Crawley
Mr. & Mrs. A. M. Dail
Col. & Mrs. David Donavan
Mrs. Jean G. Fisher
Thomas G. Fisher
J. D. & Alma Forster
Tom & Margaret Galbreath, Jr.
Mr. & Mrs. C. B. Galphin
Mr. & Mrs. Henry E. Garrison
Mrs. Marjorie M. Goodwin
Mr. & Mrs. Foy E. Grubb
Mr. & Mrs. Harold D. Hall
Mrs. Laura W. Harrill
Hatch, Little & Bunn
Mr. & Mrs. Richard Helmold
Betty & Maria Hessee
Mr. & Mrs. E. L. Hicks
Mr. & Mrs. W. E. Highsmith
Walter & Frances Hill
Mr. & Mrs. Harvey Hinnant
Carolyn S. Holding
Frank B. Holding
Waite W. Howard
Mr. & Mrs. Peter Howsam
Mr. & Mrs. Dewey H. Huffines, Jr.
N. E. Huffman
Mr. & Mrs. Worth W. Johnson
Mr. & Mrs. R. H. Kees
D. U. Kemp
Mr. & Mrs. Ben Kilgore
Koonce, Wooten & Haywood
Mr. & Mrs. John E. Koonce
Carolyn S. Leith
Mr. & Mrs. David N. Lewis
Wade & Ritchie Lewis
Dr. & Mrs. Henry Ligon
Mr. & Mrs. Fred London
Judith M. Long
Mr. & Mrs. Harold McAllister, Jr.
Mr. & Mrs. John N. McClain
Frances & John McClain, Jr.
W. W. & Lenore McClain

Henry & Sara Jo Manning
Dr. & Mrs. Isaac Manly
Mrs. Phyllis Margeson
Mrs. Walker Martin
Mr. & Mrs. W. Forest Matthews
Betsy T. Medlin
Mrs. Joseph L. Moore, Sr.
Lula Wynne Norman
Mrs. E. P. Paris
Mrs. James M. Parrott
Mrs. J. Emmett Pollock
Mr. & Mrs. James M. Poyner III
Bob & Virginia Price
Mr. & Mrs. Garth H. Quinn
Mr. & Mrs. James D. Ray, Jr
Mr. & Mrs. Richard T. Raymond
Mrs. Robert N. Simms, Jr.
Mr. & Mrs. Garland Smith
John Clayton Smith
Mr. & Mrs. Charles L. Snipes, Jr.
Mrs. Helen Starritt
Mr. & Mrs. L. O. Stevenson
Mr. & Mrs. Fred A. Stone
Mrs. John W. Thompson
Norman & Alicia Tucker
Mr. & Mrs. F. E. Wallace, Jr.
Mr. & Mrs. S. Robert Watson, Jr.
Mr. & Mrs. Van Wyck Webb
Sim & Jane Wells
David L. Ward, Jr.
R. A. Whitaker, Jr.
Beaumont Whitton Children & Spouses:
    Mary & Nick England
    Robert Whitton & Amy Diamond
    Tom & Margaret Ray
Mrs. Charles F. Williams
Jack & Betsy Willis
Cecil W. Wooten, Jr.
Mr. & Mrs. G. Smedes York

Henry Anthony McDermott, Jr.

Deb Brown
Valerie Brown
Martha Crampton
Marge Fraser

Jenny Haase
Jane Henderson
Harriet Hill
Susan Montgomery
Mary Lou Muller
Marty Munt
Margaret Nicholson
Jackie Wyche

Loved Ones of
The Carroll L. Mann, Jr. Family

Carroll L. Mann, Jr.

Allen Stancill Manning

Jack & Judy Durant
Mr. & Mrs. James Enzor
Martha N. Keravuori
Rebecca M. King
Mr. & Mrs. Alex MacFadyen
Mr. & Mrs. Harry Walker, Jr.

Tom Elbert Martin

Shirley Martin

Ed Morgan

Helen Morgan

Julia Ann Fesperman Moore

Joseph L. Moore, Jr.,
Elizabeth Ann Moore
Katherine Lewis Moore
Joseph Forrest Moore
Betty Stanley Moore
Audit Services Department:
    David G. Doughtery
    W. David Jones
    W. Ron Miller
    Judy Ricketts
    Frank Supple
Mr. & Mrs. T. Fred Armstrong
Mr. & Mrs. Fred Atkins
Mr. & Mrs. E. H. Aull
Mr. & Mrs. Donald L. Bolen, Jr.
Mr. & Mrs. Andre V. Boyette
Grover C. Boyette
Mr. & Mrs. Wyatt Brannan, Jr.
Clark C. Calvin

Ms. Betty M. Caruso
Mr. & Mrs. Barry Castle
Chase Nedrow Industries, Inc.
Mr. & Mrs. James Choate
Mr. & Mrs. Robert C. Collins
Dr. & Mrs. Maurice N. Courie
Mr. & Mrs. Gregory B. Crampton
Mr. & Mrs. Dwight Davis
Mr. & Mrs. Clarence Darling
Mr. & Mrs. John Dixon
Mr. & Mrs. William Duff, Jr.
Mr. & Mrs. William Eakes
Dr. & Mrs. F. T. Eastwood
Paul A. Emmons
John D. Farmer
Mrs. Jean G. Fisher
John T. Gallo
Mr. & Mrs. Ralph Gatling
Ann, Polly & Will Godfrey
Mr. & Mrs. Glenn Godfrey
Mr. & Mrs. John T. Green
Dr. & Mrs. Robert S. Grew
Mr. & Mrs. Richard Guirlinger
Mr. & Mrs. Boyden Hale
Mr. & Mrs. Harold Hall
Dr. & Mrs. Randolph Hall
W. F. Hamlin
Mr. & Mrs. David H. Hawes
Heimbrock, Inc.
Mr. & Mrs. W. E. Highsmith
Mr. & Mrs. Harvey J. Hinnant
Mr. & Mrs. Peter Howsam
Gary T. Hubbuch
Mr. & Mrs. Ralph B. Johnson
Mr. & Mrs. Richard F. Kane
Frank Kennedy
Mr. & Mrs. Robert Kish
Mr. & Mrs. Kenneth T. Knight
Mr. & Mrs. J. Tate Lanning
Mr. & Mrs. Fred London
Donald G. Luff
Mr. & Mrs. Richard M. McClain
Mr. & Mrs. John C. Mahler
Dr. & Mrs. Isaac V. Manly

Mr. & Mrs. Leethan N. Massey, Jr.
Mr. & Mrs. Forrest Matthews, Jr.
Metro Boiler Tube Company
Modern Refractories Service Corp.
Joe Moore and Company, Inc.
Mr. & Mrs. N. N. Moore
Mr. & Mrs. William G. Moore
Mr. & Mrs. H. Gilliam Nicholson, Jr.
Mr. & Mrs. Kenneth Oppenheim
Mr. & Mrs. J. Larkin Pahl
Mr. & Mrs. William A. Pahl, Jr.
Mr. & Mrs. Bruce V. Penwell, Jr.
Gary T. Preston
William G. Preston
Ms. Mary Anne Ragland
Mr. & Mrs. Richard T. Raymond
Mr. & Mrs. Charles Safley
St. Michael's Bookstore
Lt. Col. James W. Sanges
Schad Boiler Setting Company
Mr. & Mrs. John R. Skouse & Family
Mr. & Mrs. Dennis R. Snead, Jr.
Mr. & Mrs. Steven F. Techet
Ms. Caroline W. Thomas
Mrs. Hilda M. Tillman
Mr. & Mrs. James R. Ughrig
Utilization Management UNC
University of North Carolina Hospitals
Mr. & Mrs. William Utermohlen
Mr. & Mrs. Edwin B. Vaden, Jr.
Mr. & Mrs. Val Valentine
Mrs. Frances Vann
Mr. & Mrs. Henry B. Vess
Mrs. Roger I. Wall
John West Auto Service
Ms. Ann M. White
James Wiles
Mr. & Mrs. Mike M. Woody
Mr. & Mrs. J. W. Worley
Ms. Amanda Worth
Mr. & Mrs. G. Smedes York

Timothy Rayburn Morrison
Dr. & Mrs. Jack Durant

Hugh MacRae Morton, Jr.

Pansy Morton
Jack Morton
Crae Morton
AAA Motor Club
Mr. & Mrs. Thomas Alexander
Mr. & Mrs. William Bateman
Mr. & Mrs. Hugh Bennett, Jr.
Dr. & Mrs. Jeffrey Board
William Boles III
Mr. & Mrs. Robert Bradley
Steve & Sandra Byrd
Frank Callahan
Dr. & Mrs. Joseph Campbell
Bennett, Colin & Madeleine Campbell
Mr. & Mrs. Charles Canon
Children of Beckwith Chapel
Keith Clark
Mr. & Mrs. F. E. Cohoon
Mr. & Mrs. John Converse
Ned Covington
Mr. & Mrs. Greg Crampton
Mr. & Mrs. Dwight Davis, Ward & Quinn
Mr. & Mrs. Wright Dixon, Jr.
Mr. & Mrs. Norvin Duncan, Jr.
Maurine Elebash
William Espy
Mr. & Mrs. Richard Gammon
Mr. & Mrs. William Gideon
Rusty & Jane Goode
Keith S. Green
Mr. & Mrs. Richard Guirlinger
Boyce Hackney
Dr. & Mrs. Randolph Hall
Roxanne Hicklin
Nan Hospodar
Mr. & Mrs. Wayne Jackson
Mr. & Mrs. Lennie Jernigan
Mr. & Mrs. M. Keith Kapp
Mrs. Frank Kenan
Dr. & Mrs. Lance Landvater
Mr. & Mrs. Ronald S. Ligon
Mr. & Mrs. Robert Lincks
Cornelia McAlister

Dr. & Mrs. John McCain
Mr. & Mrs. John D. McConnell, Jr.
McGladrey & Pullen
Dr. & Mrs. Isaac Manly
Mr. & Mrs. William Marriott
Mr. & Mrs. Bruce Miller
Chris Munt
Dr. & Mrs. Robert Munt
Mr. & Mrs. Albert Myers, Jr.
Mr. & Mrs. Winston Page, Jr.
Mr. & Mrs. William Perdew
Mr. & Mrs. Ralph Peters
Dr. & Mrs. Lloyd Peterson
Marie H. Perry
Mr. & Mrs. William Prewitt
Mr. & Mrs. Robert Price
Becky V. Rose
Mr. & Mrs. Charles Safley
Chris Safley
SAS Institute
Greg Shank
Mrs. P. R. Smith
S. H. Smith, Jr.
Mr. & Mrs. David Sousa
Mr. & Mrs. Russell W. Travison
Peter & Harriet Vanstory
Harry, Linda, Lee & Louisa Walker
Mrs. Roger Wall
Mr. & Mrs. Peyton Watson
Dave & Judy Whichard
Dennis Wicker Committee
Mr. & Mrs. Edward Williams
Diana Witt
Mr. & Mrs. Mike Zafirovski

Harold Motz
Mr. & Mrs. Aldert Root Edmonson

Harrison Gray Otis, Jr.
Nancy E. Titus

William Arthur Pahl, Sr.
Roxanna G. Pahl
Mr. & Mrs. Jose Almaraz
Mr. & Mrs. William Bateman
Dr. & Mrs. Vladimir Bensen

Robert & Lynda Boone
The Rev. Lawrence K. Brown
Mildred Bryant
Bull & Bear Society
Mr. & Mrs. William A. Bullard
Campbell & Logsdon
Frank T. Colvert
Mr. & Mrs. Gregory Crampton
Mr. & Mrs. Frank Cranor
Stig Dahlstrom
Mrs. Betty Duff
Mr. & Mrs. Oscar Elmore
Nancy F. Fadum
Faison & Brown
Thomas G. Fisher
Rebecca H. Glass
Mr. & Mrs. Harold Hall
Mr. & Mrs. James A. Hill, Jr.
Azile G. Honaker
Mrs. & Mrs. Jim Ingram
Mr. & Mrs. William Ingram
Jackson Painting Company, Inc.
Johnson Communications & Electronics
Mr. & Mrs. Walter Keezell
King's Auto Service
Mr. & Mrs. Kenneth Knight
William C. Lawton
Lincoln Developers
Mr. & Mrs. Jim Lister
Richard C. McElroy III
Dr. & Mrs. Isaac Manly
Mrs. Phyllis Margeson
Mr. & Mrs. W. Forrest Matthews, Jr.
Mr. & Mrs. Fred Meisenheimer
Mrs. Jean Mercer
Mitchell Puryear Jedco Contruction
    Company
Mr. & Mrs. J. L. Moore, Sr.
Mr. & Mrs. Gilliam Nicholson, Jr.
Mr. & Mrs. H. Gilliam Nicholson, Sr.
North Carolina National Bank
Mr. & Mrs. James B. Nourse
Mrs. Eleanor Overten
Dr. & Mrs. Hayne Palmour
Linda Pitts

Quota Club of Raleigh
Mr. & Mrs. James E. Rackley
Mr. & Mrs. Garland Radford
Robert J. Ramseur
Mrs. Marguerite P. Reeve
Mr. & Mrs. Greg Roberts
Mrs. Marian N. Roberts
Kenneth R. Shaker
Mr. & Mrs. David Shelburne
St. Michael's Episcopal Church
St. Michael's Episcopal Young Churchmen
Smith, Debnam, Hibbert & Pahl, LLP
Mr. & Mrs. Fred J. Smith, Jr.
Mrs. Fred Smith, Sr.
John Clayton Smith
Mr. & Mrs. Steve Techet
Dr. John F. Vaughan
Mrs. Roger I. Wall
Mr. & Mrs. Earle Wood, Jr.
Mr. & Mrs. Francis Welles
Dale P. Williams
Mr. & Mrs. Douglas Williams
F. Carter Williams
Hal Worth
Mr. & Mrs. Hunter Wyche, Jr.

Mary Duttera Parker
Betsy Parker Wray

Caryn Reed
Kathleen F. Hogg

Donald Wayne Roberts
St. Michael's Senior Choir

Edwin Rochelle
Mrs. Nell Rochelle

Margaret Moore Senter
James Pearce and Margaret Moore Senter

Margaret Darst Smith
John Clayton Smith
Margaret Smith Timberlake
John Clayton Smith, Jr.
Mr. & Mrs. Thomas F. Adams
Mr. & Mrs. Richard S. Andrews
Mr. & Mrs. Ned B. Ball

C. Lynn Banks, Real Estate
Phyllis Bates
Mrs. Marjorie F. Berson
Beaver Dam Lake, Inc.
Mr. & Mrs. Charles Blanchard
Mr. & Mrs. Robert Boyles
Lalla C. Bragaw
Mr. & Mrs. Micou F. Browne
Ruth A. Browning
Mr. & Mrs. Douglas Bryant
Mrs. Barbara Buchanan
Charles E. & Deborah L. Casey
Mr. & Mrs. Bruce Cauthen
Maydwelle M. Coleman
Mr. & Mrs. Lenox Cooper, Jr.
Lenox S. Cooper, Sr.
Mr. & Mrs. G. K. Core
Dr. & Mrs. Maurice N. Courie
Mr. & Mrs. Oliver Crawley
Clarence R. & Barbara B. Darling
Laura Debnam
Mr. & Mrs. W. L. Dempsey
Elizabeth D. DeMent
Mr. & Mrs. Wright T. Dixon, Jr.
Edward N. & Jeanette S. Dunn
Mr. & Mrs. John Farmer
Elizabeth T. Gauss
Mr. & Mrs. Karl Graetz
Mr. & Mrs. Robert Greene
Bob Greer
Worth P. & Elizabeth B. Gurley
Mr. & Mrs. Harold Hall
Mrs. Nelda Harris
Mr. & Mrs. Vernon O. Harris, Jr.
Mr. & Mrs. F. B. Hart
Mr. & Mrs. Miles Higgins
Mr. & Mrs. William Holloman
George B. & Rebecca W. Holdsworth
Mrs. Sidney S. Holt
Mr. & Mrs. Peter Howsam
Louise W. Hutchinson
Mr. & Mrs. Herbert Jackson
Mr. & Mrs. E. B. Jeffress, Jr.
Mr. & Mrs. Kenneth Knight
Mr. & Mrs. J. Tate Lanning, Jr.

Dr. Sarah Lemmon
Mrs. Henry Ligon
Mr. & Mrs. Fred London
Mr. & Mrs. George London
Raleigh Office Building Employees &
    Wallman Family
Mr. & Mrs. Ellis Lundy
Mr. & Mrs. Harold McAllister
Mr. & Mrs. Richard McClain
Mrs. Ruth L. McClam
Tricia McClam
William P. & Cornelia A. McPherson
Dr. & Mrs. Isaac Manly
William J. & Cynthia Maroney
Mrs. H. Way Marsh
Mr. & Mrs. W. Forrest Matthews, Jr.
Mrs. Joseph L. Moore
Patricia Ann Moore
Mr. & Mrs. Richard Myers
Mr. & Mrs. H. Gilliam Nicholson
Mr. & Mrs. Herbert E. O'Keefe, Jr.
Dr. & Mrs. Hayne Palmour III
John A., Jr. & Julia A. Park
Mr. & Mrs. Bruce Penwell
Charles A. Poe
George Smedes Poyner Foundation, Inc.
Mr. & Mrs. Garland Radford
Mr. & Mrs. Richard Raymond
Mr. & Mrs. Reddids Revelle
Mrs. Edwin C. Rochelle
St. Michael's Episcopal Church
Kindergarten
Mary Boney Sheats
Mr. & Mrs. Edgar Smith
Col. & Mrs. Wesley P. Smith
David S. Sparrow
Jane C. Stafford
Mr. & Mrs. Norwood Starling
Mrs. Helen Starritt
Col & Mrs. R. E. Timberlake
Jennie D. Todd
Mr. & Mrs. John Tropman
Mr. & Mrs. Charles Tucker, Jr.
Mrs. Roger I. Wall
Mr. & Mrs. Van Wyck Webb

Mr. & Mrs. Don Wesen
Mr. & Mrs. Charles Williams
Mr. & Mrs. Emerson Willard
Dr. & Mrs. Francis Winslow
Mr. & Mrs. P. Earle Wood
Griselle Gholson Woodward
The Rt. Rev. & Mrs. Thomas Wright
Maria Alston Young

Marie Cohen Smith

Woodford L. & Pamela Smith Burnette
Mr. & Mrs. W. Davidson Call
Mr. & Mrs. Dwight Davis
Dr. & Mrs. Jack Durant
Mr. & Mrs. Root Edmonson
Burnette Herrick
Mr. & Mrs. Harry Hurd
Mrs. Betty Moore
Mr. & Mrs. Spears Mullen
Mr. & Mrs. Bruce Muller
Mr. & Mrs. David Sendall
Mr. & Mrs. Peter J. Swenson
Mr. & Mrs. John Temple

Joseph John Spaziano and Dorothy Townsend Spaziano Fisher

Robert Townsend & Judith Lawton
  Spaziano

Sara Spurlin

Mrs. Betty Moore

Margaret Green Taylor

Gilbert S. Taylor
David & Rick Taylor
Mrs. Margaret Belvin
Mr. & Mrs. Charles Blanchard
Dr. & Mrs. Jack Durant
Mary Lou Ellis
Mrs. Jean Fisher
Mr. & Mrs. A. E. Fussell
Mr. & Mrs. Robert Greene
Mrs. Elizabeth Johnston
Mrs. J. L. Moore
Mrs. Robert C. Nesmith
Mr. & Mrs. Jack Norwood

Allen Robert Tomlinson

James A., Jr. & Harriet Tomlinson Hill
James Allen III & Charles Martin Hill

The Rev. Richard Turkleson

Mrs. Roger I. Wall

Andrew David Trask

David Knowlton & Barbara Bennett Trask
Robert Bennett Trask
John Douglas Trask
Mr. & Mrs. Robert Collins
Jack & Judy Durant
Martha N. Keravuori
Harry & Sallie Walker

Claire Twomey

Mr. & Mrs. Charles Blanchard

Elizabeth Utermohlen

Mr. & Mrs. Wright Dixon, Jr.

Mark Utermohlen

Don & Elaine Bell
Mr. & Mrs. J. M. Broughton III
Jack & Barbara Bush
Mr. & Mrs. Harry Caldwell
Mr. & Mrs. William P. Gearhart
Mrs. Jean Graves
Mr. & Mrs. Robert C. Greene, Sr.
Mr. & Mrs. Boyden Hale
Doris Ann Holden
Mr. & Mrs. Vinton A. Hoyl, Jr.
Dr. & Mrs. LeRoy F. Kenan
Mary Fran Lyman
Mr. & Mrs. A. E. Martens
John A. Milhop
Mr. & Mrs. W. Forrest Matthews, Jr.
Mrs. J. L. Moore, Sr.
Raleigh Creative Costumes

Frank Wagoner

St. Michael's Senior Choir

Luther Wagoner

Mr. & Mrs. E. Alan Bishop

Roger Irving Wall
Phyllis Stier Wall
Audrey Wall Black

Florence Fields Ward
her son, Henry Vance Ward, Jr. and
his sons, Andrew O. Ward &
    Henry G. Ward

Lewis P. Watson
Mr. & Mrs. James A. Hill, Jr.
Mrs. Roger I. Wall

Samuel Robert Watson, Jr.
Lillian Harward Watson
Samuel Robert Watson III
Bettie Watson Toma
Jane Watson Rigsbee
Mary Lois Eakes
Mrs. & Mrs. James Black
Mr. & Mrs. Wright Dixon, Jr.
The Garden Friends
Dr. & Mrs. Randolph Hall
Mrs. J. L. Moore

Van Wyck Hoke Webb
Mr. & Mrs. James B. Black III
Mr. & Mrs. Gregory B. Crampton
Mr. & Mrs. Wright Dixon, Jr.
Dr. & Mrs. Randolph Hall
Mr. & Mrs. James A. Hill, Jr.
Mr. & Mrs. Winston L. Page, Jr.
Mrs. Don E. Scott, Jr.
Mrs. Lillian Watson

Earl Tyler Welch
Mrs. Sally Ramsey

John T. Welch
Mary Leona Ruffin Welch
Gwendolyn C. Barger
Big Brothers & Sisters of Greater
    Jacksonville, Fla.
Micou F. Browne
Barbara W. Buchanan
Harry W. Candler, Jr.
Mr. & Mrs. Robert C. Collins

Mrs. Oliver C. Crawley
Mr. & Mrs. Dwight L. Dixon
Mr. & Mrs. R. T. Edmonson
H. H. Haines
Mr. & Mrs. Ben Hassoun
Mr. & Mrs. Peter Howsam
Elizabeth T. Johns
Mrs. Worth Johnson
Mr. & Mrs. Kenneth Knight
Barbara W. Linder
Mr. & Mrs. Fred London
Mr. & Mrs. Robert E. Long
Mr. & Mrs. Wiley McNeil, Jr.
Orlando Urology Association
Mr. & Mrs. Richard Raymond
Mrs. Edwin Rochelle
Mrs. Helen Starritt
Mrs. Phyllis S. Wall
Mr. & Mrs. Van Wyck Webb
W. E. Wooten

Thomas B. Willard
Mrs. Marjorie Goodwin

Betty V. Williams
Mr. & Mrs. Wright Dixon, Jr.

Walter Williams
Mr. & Mrs. Winston L. Page, Jr.

Millard Mial and
    Suzanne Gillon Williamson
Thomas Mial & Lisa Cooke Williamson

Reverdy and Nancy Winfree
Reverdy, Jr. & Judy Edmonson Winfree
    & family

Nettie Gresham Wood
W. Robert Pollard

P. Earle Wood, Jr.
Jim & Harriet Hill

Benjamin Watson Woodruff
Leon, Bonnie & Molly Woodruff
Mr. & Mrs. Keith Allen
Mr. & Mrs. Jack Andrews

Mr. & Mrs. William Bateman
Mr. & Mrs. Jim Black
Mr. & Mrs. Charles Blanchard
Mr. & Mrs. Andy Boyette
Mr. & Mrs. Woodford Burnette
Dr. & Mrs. Joseph Campbell
Mr. & Mrs. Robert Collins
Mr. & Mrs. John Converse
Dr. & Mrs. Maurice N. Courie
Mr. & Mrs. Greg Crampton
Mr. & Mrs. Charles Culpepper
Mary B. Currin
Mr. & Mrs. David Daniel
Mr. & Mrs. Dwight Davis
Mr. & Mrs. Wright T. Dixon, Jr.
Mr. & Mrs. William Duff III
Dr. & Mrs. Jack D. Durant
Mr. & Mrs. Root Edmonson
Mr. & Mrs. Jimmy Enzor
Neil & Ann Evans
John Farmer
Mr. & Mrs. M. L. Finch, Jr.
Mrs. Jean Fisher
Mr. & Mrs. Glenn Godfrey
Mr. & Mrs. Harold Hall
Mr. & Mrs. Burt Harden
Mr. & Mrs. A. E. Harer
Mr. & Mrs. Burke Haywood
Mr. & Mrs. Richard Henderson
Mr. & Mrs. Wilbur E. Highsmith
Mr. & Mrs. James A. Hill, Jr.
Kathleen Hogg
Mr. & Mrs. William Ingram
Mrs. Edith G. Jack
Travis L. Jackson
Martha Jenkins
Mimi Keravuori
Rebecca M. King
Koinonia Group
Mr. & Mrs. Fred London
Dr. & Mrs. Lance Landvater
Marguerite MacNelly
Mr. & Mrs. Alex MacFadyen, Jr.
Dr. & Mrs. Isaac Manly

Mrs. Phyllis Margeson
Mrs. J. L. Moore
Mr. & Mrs. Spears Mullen
Mr. & Mrs. Bruce Muller
Dr. & Mrs. Robert Munt, Jr.
Mr. & Mrs. H. Gilliam Nicholson, Jr.
Mr. & Mrs. Winston Page
Mr. & Mrs. William A. Pahl, Jr.
Dr. & Mrs. Hayne Palmour
Robin L. Peacock
Whit & Buffa Powell
Pregnancy Life Care
Mr. & Mrs. William Prewitt
Mr. & Mrs. Garland Radford
Mr. & Mrs. Lindsay Reed
David & Diana Sendall
Mr. & Mrs. G. A. Smith
Gretchen Smith
Mr. & Mrs. David Sousa
Mr. & Mrs. Norwood Starling
Dr. & Mrs. Arthur Stone
Mr. & Mrs. John D. Titchener, Jr.
Dr. & Mrs. Sameh K. Toma
Harry & Sally Walker
Harry, Linda, Lee & Louisa Walker
Mrs. Phyllis Wall
Marian Weatherspoon
Paul & Sara White
Dr. & Mrs. Francis Winslow
Mr. & Mrs. Hal Worth III
Beacham & Betsy Wray, Chad & Will
   Davis
Mr. & Mrs. Smedes York

Ala Yow
Mr. & Mrs. Greg Crampton
Dr. & Mrs. Randolph Hall
Dr. & Mrs. Isaac Manly

In Honor of:

Durwood W. and Evelyn D. Adams
James M., Jr. & Nancy Adams Boyette

Kelly & Sarah Basham
Jane R. Stikeleather

Francis and Phyllis Cooke
Thomas Mial & Lisa Cooke Williamson

Maurice N. Courie
Bobbi Otis Courie

Elizabeth McNinch Currin
Ellen Corbitt Currin
Mac & Mary B. Currin

Maj. (Ret.) Robert and
Fleta Edmonson
Reverdy & Judy Edmonson Winfree
& Family

Marjorie Rimbach Fraser
(Gifts listed "In Memory of The Rt. Rev.
Thomas A. Fraser, Jr.")

James West Good
Keith E. & Sue Ann Allen
Nanci K. Atkeson
Beckwith Choir:
Bill Bateman
Roger Black
Craig Cadwallader
Katherine Caldwell
Anna Crampton
Robert Davis
Ben Garren
Michael Guerrero
Scott Guirlinger
Alice Hager
Mary Lovell Hall
Evans Kistler
Alison Lighthall
Dorothy Meiburg
Jenny Page
Amy Rickman
Chad Rickman
Benjamin Rush
Jonathan Starritt
Demeree Stone
Fred Stone
Matthew Whited
Hunt Wyche

Jim & Nancy Boyette
Mo & Bobbi Courie
Greg & Martha Crampton
Dwight & Sandra Davis
Jimbo & Frances G. Dempsey
Neil & Anne Evans
Mel & Nell Finch
Amy Good
John & Genie Haley
Randy & Beth Hall
Jim & Harriet Hill
Allen, Martin & Robert Hill
Becky King
Lee & Mary Lou Lively
Stan, Catherine & Jonathan Meiburg
Bruce & Mary Lou Muller
Gilliam & Margaret Nicholson
Happy Olmstead
Billy & Martha Pahl
Larkin & Alice Pahl
Jamie, Kevin, Chris, Allison & Caddy Pahl
Hayne & Barbara Palmour
Michael & Melissa Raley
Chuck & Mary Smith
Ellen M. Smith
Timothy N. Smith
Terry & Elsie Thomas
Bill & Gail Waters

Jack and Lillian Holding Lawton
Robert Townsend & Judith Lawton
Spaziano

Mr. and Mrs. Wade Lewis
The Christian Foundation

Betsy Tingley McClain
(Gifts listed "In Memory of Richard
Marvin McClain")

Michael David and
Kelly Elizabeth Sousa
Mr. & Mrs. David Sousa

In Thanksgiving for:

Christy Cannon Lorgan
Theresa Cannon Scornavacchi
Colbert Hanchett Cannon
Woodward & Helen Christy Cannon

James Allen Hill III
Charles Martin Hill
James A., Jr. & Harriet Tomlinson Hill

Little Angels, Beckwith and
Canterbury Choirs
Ray & Trudy Bennett

Mary Katherine Bell
James Sawyer Manly
Elizabeth Fern Jernigan
Margaret Louise Graddy
Children of Dr. & Mrs. Isaac Vaughn
Manly

Patricia Senter Williams
Carol Senter Evans
James Pearce & Margaret Moore Senter

Phyllis Stier Wall
James B. & Audrey Wall Black
Jamie, Peyton & Roger Black

Ronald Hughes and
Phyllis Wall Purdy
Ronald Hunt Purdy
Louise Purdy Pardon
Roger Wall Purdy

L. Randolph and Linda Wall Isley
Philip Randolph Isley
Elizabeth Ashley Isley
James Bell III and
Audrey Wall Black
James Bell Black IV
Peyton Randolph Black
Roger Ashley Black
Barbara Wall Fraser
Jessica Patricia Fraser
Madeline Wall Fraser
Children & Grandchildren of
Phyllis Stier Wall

For Service and Devotion Rendered to
St. Michael's Episcopal Church:

The Rev. Dr. Charles M. Riddle III
Erma Dance Riddle
The Rev. Claudia A. Dickson
Lyman & Maria Kiser

To The Glory of God:
Dr. & Mrs. Vladimir B. Bensen
Catherine A. Dearstyne
Mr. & Mrs. James R. Jones
Mr. & Mrs. Fred W. London
St. Michael's Episcopal Church Women
Tim & Cathy Stewart
Audrey Valone
Elizabeth Wray
William M. Ingram

History of St. Michael's Episcopal Church

At the North Carolina Diocesan Convention in May 1947, Bishop Edwin A. Penick urged communities in larger cities to start new residential missions. In January 1948, at the congregational meeting of the Church of the Good Shepherd, the Rev. James McDowell Dick, Rector, presented the need and the opportunity for a new Episcopal parish in Raleigh. The last mission in the Raleigh area, St. Saviour's (now St. Timothy's), had been established in the late 1800's by Christ Episcopal Church. Since that time, the population of Raleigh had doubled. A committee, composed of members from Good Shepherd, St. Saviour's and Christ Church, was appointed to formulate a mission in northwest Raleigh. Plans were held in abeyance for two years because St. Saviour's was to become a parish.

On February 10, 1950, a meeting of 75 people from the three Raleigh churches agreed to help establish a new mission. The charter for St. Michael's mission was signed by 118 people on April 16, 1950, in the Chapel of St. Mary's College. By early May 1950, the charter list reached 165. Bishop Penick appointed the following members of the new congregation to the Mission Committee:

> John A. Park, Jr., Warden, R. Lee Covington, William Dunn, Jr.,
> J.C.B. Ehringhaus III, J. MacDuff, James M. Poyner, Fred W. Reebals,
> John Clayton Smith, Dr. Alex Webb, Jr., Dr. Charles F. Williams,
> Hal V. Worth, and J. Willie York.

St. Mary's Chapel was offered as a temporary place of worship, and the Rev. I. Harding Hughes, chaplain at St. Mary's, served as temporary priest-in-charge, conducting the first service of St. Michael's mission on the evening of May 6, 1950.

In May of 1950, the site committee announced a gift of a 4.5 acre lot on Canterbury Road by charter members, Mary Smedes Poyner and James Wesley "Willie" York, and temporary buildings were provided by Mr. York and E. N. Richards. Bishop Penick officiated at the first service held in the (almost completed) "little red church in the woods" on Sunday morning, September 10, 1950. Mrs. John A. Park, Jr. provided a nursery in her home to enable the large number of parishioners with young children to attend the service.

After a great deal of prayer and research, the church issued a call to the Rev. James Dunbar Beckwith, who assumed duties as the first rector of St. Michael's on October 1, 1950. He and his wife, Elizabeth, arrived at a mission with few members, no rectory and no budget but with faith and optimism for the future.

St. Michael's was granted full parish status in May 1951, and soon outgrew its temporary buildings. Three additions were constructed during the first five years, and in December 1955, the congregation included 641 baptized members and 421 confirmed communicants. With $75,000 in the building fund, $100,000 borrowed by the vestry, and $50,000 anticipated in pledges, parishioners broke ground for a permanent structure on December 26, 1955. Architect Lief Valand, a charter member of St. Michael's, designed the building, and the cornerstone was laid in November 1956. That year, on Christmas Eve, the first midnight service of the Holy Eucharist was held in the new church.

On September 4, 1958, Mrs. Carroll Mann and Mr. Beckwith established St. Michael's Kindergarten, as a service to the community.

The 15-year construction loan was repaid in nine years, and the mortgage burned on the fourteenth anniversary of the parish. May 3, 1970, marked the first use of a newly completed parish hall, and on the church's twenty-fifth anniversary, that hall was named in honor of James Dunbar Beckwith.

By the fall of 1977, a 2,412-pipe Moller organ was dedicated and in late 1982 extensive renovations were made to the educational and choir facilities.

As Christ Church and The Church of the Good Shepherd had done before, St. Michael's responded to an expanding city. In December 1985, its members helped to established a parochial mission, the Church of the Nativity, which became a full parish on January 29, 1994.

A five-year project to install stained glass windows in the nave of the church was completed and dedicated on June 7, 1987. All windows were tributes given by parishioners. Work continued toward completion of the chapel and narthex windows.

In the spring of 1990, St. Michael's broke ground for a Habitat for Humanity house. After hundreds of hours, many fund raisers, numerous aches and pains and a communion of saints, "our" young family, the Buonyas, moved to their new home in August, and a glorious celebration of dedication was held in September.

A Canterbury Road house adjacent to St. Michael's was purchased in 1991, and, following a Capital Campaign (to refurbish the new acquisition, to retire debts and to establish a capital reserve fund), in 1995 the house became the main gathering place for the youth of the parish.

By 1997, the numerous outreach and parish programs of the church continued to thrive; the chapel and narthex windows were installed, and St. Michael's was blessed with a vibrant membership of over 2,000, a new rector and a growing congregation that joyously anticipated a new century in God's service.

Past and Present Clergy

1950-1977	The Reverend James D. Beckwith, Rector
1960-1963	The Reverend Leland Shuttuck Jamieson, Jr., Assistant to the Rector
1965-1971	The Reverend Thomas Cecil Walker, Assistant to the Rector
1972-1977	The Reverend Lawrence K. Brown, Assistant Rector
1977-1995	The Reverend Lawrence K. Brown, Rector
1977-1982	The Reverend Douglas E. Remer, Assistant Rector
1979-1982	The Reverend James L. Hutton III, Outreach Programs
1983-1987	The Reverend Gary L. Cline, Assistant Rector
1987-1994	The Reverend Dwight E. Ogier, Jr., Assistant Rector
1986-1989	The Right Reverend Thomas A. Fraser, Jr., Bishop-in-Residence
1989-1995	The Reverend M. Blair Both, Assistant Rector
1994-	The Reverend Claudia A. Dickson, Assistant Rector
1995-1997	The Reverend Dr. Charles M. Riddle III, Interim Rector
1997-	The Reverend George Kenneth Grant Henry, Rector

St. Michael's Episcopal Church

1520 Canterbury Road
Raleigh, North Carolina 27608
(919) 782-0731

The Right Reverend Robert Johnson, Jr., D.D.
Bishop of North Carolina

The Right Reverend J. Gary Gloster, D.D.
Bishop Suffragan

The Reverend George Kenneth Grant Henry
Rector

The Reverend Claudia A. Dickson
Associate Rector

Dr. James W. Good
Organist/Choirmaster

Priscilla Laite
Director, Religious Education

M. Benjamin Gaddy
Youth Ministry

D. Carol Johnson
Business/Systems Administrator

Marina Strawser
Rector's Secretary

Susan W. Little
Financial Secretary

M. Lea Batts
Publications Editor

Biographical Data

Researcher

A native of Florence, Alabama, Harriet Tomlinson Hill earned a Bachelor of Music Degree in 1961 from Salem College, Winston-Salem, North Carolina. After her marriage in 1964, she moved from Atlanta to Raleigh and has been a communicant at St. Michael's since 1973. She is a lifelong Episcopalian and has been involved in many aspects of the Church. Since moving to Raleigh, she has been treasurer of the Episcopal Churchwomen of the Diocese of North Carolina, has been active as a member of the Adult Choir and the Episcopal Churchwomen at St. Michael's, has served on the Vestry and was Junior Warden in 1984. Harriet Hill's activites in the schools and in the community have been numerous. A published author, she is married to James A. Hill, Jr., a C.P.A., and they have three children, Allen, Martin and Robert.

Author of Nave Window Script

The son and grandson of navy chaplains, Dr. James F. Day earned degrees from Stetson University and the University of Florida. He later went to Oxford University to read history and took an M.A. in 1982, while he was working on a Ph.D. in English Literature at Duke University.

Before completing the Ph.D. in 1985, James Day became involved in the stained glass windows project at St. Michael's, serving as a consultant in iconography, an interest that closely parallels his dissertation research on heraldry and literature. Aside from writing the commentary on the nave windows in this guide, he also suggested the present arrangement of the windows in an order commemorating the church year.

The Artist

The artist-designer of the windows, Mary Patricia Stumpf, is a native of Acquilla, Missouri. She studied Art and English at Southern Illinois University, where she began to specialize in what has become her most frequent art medium, batik.* She later continued her art studies at the Art Institute in Chicago. She is married to Dale R. Stumpf, and they have a son, Brice. They now reside in Raleigh, North Carolina.

For more than a decade, Patricia Stumpf's work has been featured in one-woman exhibits in Richmond, Tampa, St. Louis, Charlotte, Raleigh, and in Japan. She has shown works— and garnished important Awards—in a number of juried exhibits of national and international stature held in major U.S. cities, including New York, Washington, Los Angeles and

---

* An inherent understanding of composition and design coupled with a thorough knowledge of color gained through the batik experience (unknowingly) prepared her for dealing with the special design constraints—and opportunities—encountered in working with stained glass.

Boston. She has produced a number of commissioned works for industrial, institutional and private collectors.

Patricia Stumpf is a member of the National League of American Pen Women, and the Women's Club of Raleigh. As visting artist, lecturer and teacher, she has taken an active role in bringing art and the art experience directly into the classroom and the community.

When queried about her deep personal involvement in creating coordinated designs for the stained glass windows of St. Michael's, she cited this quotation: "Among the innumerable thoughts and fancies that pass through your mind and the imagination without any trace, there are some which leave a deep, pronounced groove so that often when you no longer remember the essence of thought, you are conscious that something good has been in your mind, you feel the trace of the thought and try to reproduce it."†

She says, "I feel this way about my faith, and believe it is reflected in the windows."

The Stained Glass Studio

The Willet Stained Glass Studios Inc. was founded in 1898 by William Willet. His son, Henry Lee Willet, and grandson, E. Crosby Willet, have carried on the traditions and ownership of the company. In 1977, the company was sold to Hauser Studios in Winona, Minnesota, but Crosby Willet remains the president of the studio in Philadelphia.

The thousands of Willet's windows found throughout the United States and in many foreign countries include the chapel in the Military Academy at West Point, at Princeton University, Ohio State University, the National Cathedral in Washington, D.C., the Cathedral of St. John the Divine in New York City, and the chapel of the Church Center at the United Nations. It was its long-standing reputation for fine craftsmanship that led to the commissioning of Willet Studios for the fabrication of *our* long-awaited Windows of St. Michael's.

---

† Tolstoy —*From Boyhood*